Δ The Triangle Papers: 44

INTERNATIONAL MIGRATION CHALLENGES IN A NEW ERA

POLICY PERSPECTIVES AND PRIORITIES FOR
EUROPE, JAPAN, NORTH AMERICA
AND THE INTERNATIONAL COMMUNITY

A Report to
The Trilateral Commission

Authors: DORIS M. MEISSNER
Director, Immigration Policy Project,
Carnegie Endowment for International Peace
Washington, D.C.

ROBERT D. HORMATS
Vice Chairman, Goldman Sachs International,
Goldman, Sachs & Co.
New York City

ANTONIO GARRIGUES WALKER
Senior Partner, J&A Garrigues; Special Advisor
to the UN High Commissioner for Refugees
Madrid

SHIJURO OGATA
Former Deputy Governor for International
Relations, Bank of Japan
Tokyo

published by
The Trilateral Commission
New York, Paris and Tokyo
1993

Library of Congress Cataloging-in-Publication Data

International Migration Challenges in a New Era: Policy Perspectives
   and Priorities for Europe, Japan, North America and the
   International Community: a report to the Trilateral Commission/
   Doris M. Meissner... [et. al.].

     p. cm. — (The Triangle papers : 44)
ISBN 0-930503-69-4 : $12.00
1. Emigration and immigration. 2. Emigration and immigration-
Government policy.
I. Meissner, Doris, M. II. Trilateral Commission. III. Series.
JV6091.I57 1993
325—dc20
                                         93-30078
                                           CIP

Manufactured in the United States of America

THE TRILATERAL COMMISSION

345 East 46th Street
New York, NY 10017

c/o Japan Center for
International Exchange
4-9-17 Minami-Azabu
Minato-ku
Tokyo, Japan

35, avenue de Friedland
75008 Paris, France

The Authors

DORIS M. MEISSNER (drafter of report) was nominated by President Clinton to become Commissioner of the U.S. Immigration and Naturalization Service (INS) in June 1993, shortly after completing this report. Since 1986 she has been Director of the Immigration Policy Project at the Carnegie Endowment for International Peace. Educated at the University of Wisconsin (B.A., 1963, and M.A., 1969), Ms. Meissner was a White House Fellow in the Attorney General's office in 1973-74. She worked in several other capacities in the Justice Department, including as Deputy Associate Attorney General in 1977-80, and then joined the INS in 1981, serving as Acting Commissioner, Acting Deputy Commissioner, and Executive Associate Commissioner, until leaving government service in 1986.

ROBERT D. HORMATS (project chairman) joined Goldman, Sachs & Co. in 1982, where he is now Vice Chairman of Goldman Sachs International. Educated at Tufts University (B.S., 1965) and the Fletcher School of Law and Diplomacy (M.A. and Ph.D., 1970), Mr. Hormats has had extensive experience in the U.S. government—as Senior Staff Member for Economic Affairs at the National Security Council (1969-73, 1974-77), as Deputy Assistant Secretary of State for Economic and Business Affairs (1977-79), as Ambassador and Deputy U.S. Trade Representative (1979-81), and as Assistant Secretary of State for Economic and Business Affairs (1981-82).

ANTONIO GARRIGUES WALKER is a Senior Partner of J & A Garrigues, a law firm with offices in Madrid, Barcelona, Brussels and New York. He is a Special Advisor to the United Nations High Commissioner for Refugees, a Vice President of Liberal International, and a former Chairman of the World Association of Lawyers.

SHIJURO OGATA has spent most of his career (1950-86) with the Bank of Japan, serving as Deputy Governor for International Affairs in 1984-86. He was Deputy Governor of the Japan Development Bank in 1986-91, and is now a Senior Advisor to Yamaichi Securities. Educated at the University of Tokyo (Faculty of Law, graduated in 1950) and the Fletcher School of Law and Diplomacy, Mr. Ogata is also the husband of Sadako Ogata, the United Nations High Commissioner for Refugees. He was one of the authors of a 1989 report to the Trilateral Commission entitled *International Financial Integration: The Policy Challenges.*

The Trilateral Process

The report which follows is the joint responsibility of the four authors. It was written by Doris Meissner.

This project began in 1991-92 with a Trilateral Commission working group on migration and refugee issues, also chaired by Robert Hormats. Doris Meissner was one of several experts and Trilateral members who prepared individual papers for the working group. These papers were discussed at a workshop in New York City in early 1992. Mr. Hormats then prepared an "Interim Note" for the wider Trilateral membership, which was the basis for a discussion at the April 1992 annual meeting in Lisbon. The Hormats "Interim Note" and various individual papers were subsequently published by the Trilateral Commission in a volume entitled *Working Group Papers 1991-92*. The 1991-92 elements of this project were generously supported by the Japan Foundation Center for Global Partnership.

The 1992-93 stage of this project, generously supported by the Andrew W. Mellon Foundation, has focused on preparation of the current report. Consultations have been particularly active in Europe. Antonio Garrigues Walker and Paul Révay met on three occasions with the "Brussels Group" at UNHCR in Brussels — on June 29 and September 9, 1992, and on January 20, 1993. A number of European members participated in a workshop with the authors in Dublin on October 25-26, 1992, just after the fall meeting of the Trilateral Commission's European Group. The authors also gathered in Geneva on February 8-9, 1993, and used the occasion for some outside consultation as well as for detailed discussion of chapters of the report. In North America, Doris Meissner met with a number of Canadian members and government officials in Ottawa on December 3, 1992. Robert Hormats and Doris Meissner discussed the draft report with a number of North American experts and members in Washington, D.C., on February 16, 1993.

A full draft of this report was the basis for a discussion at the 1993 annual meeting of the Trilateral Commission, held on March 27-29 in Washington, D.C. Some others provided useful comments in the weeks following the Washington meeting. Final refinements before publication were completed in June 1993, shortly before President Clinton nominated Doris Meissner to be the new head of the U.S. Immigration and Naturalization Service (INS).

The Trilateral Commission particularly appreciates the help and inspiration provided all along the way during this project by Sadako Ogata, United Nations High Commissioner for Refugees. Mrs. Ogata spoke at the April 1991 (in Tokyo) and April 1992 (in Lisbon) annual meetings of the Commission, and at the October 1992 meeting of the European group. The authors of this report consulted with her in Geneva on February 8, 1993.

Although only the authors are responsible for the analysis and conclusions, they have been aided in their work by many others in the above meetings and other consultations. The persons consulted spoke for themselves as individuals and not as representatives of any institution with which they are associated. Those consulted or otherwise assisting in the development of the report include the following:

Ruprecht von Arnim, *Regional Delegate, Regional Office for the European Institutions, UNHCR, Brussels*

Paul Balaran, *Program Officer, International Affairs, Ford Foundation*

Piero Bassetti, *Chairman, Chamber of Commerce and Industry, Milan; former Member of the Italian Chamber of Deputies*

Ritt Bjerregaard, *Member of the Danish Parliament; Chairman, Social Democratic Parliamentary Group; former Minister of Education and Minister for Social Affairs*

Gerald K. Bouey, *Former Governor of the Bank of Canada*

Richard Conroy, *Chairman, Conroy Petroleum; Member of the Senate, Irish Republic*

Alain Cotta, *Professor of Economics and Management, University of Paris*

Ian Deans, *Chairperson of the Public Service Relations Board of Canada*

Jean Deflassieux, *Chairman, Banque des Echanges Internationaux; Honorary Chairman, Crédit Lyonnais, Paris*

Robert DeVecchi, *Executive Director, International Rescue Committee, New York*

Peter C. Dobell, *Director, Parliamentary Centre for Foreign Affairs and Foreign Trade, Ottawa*

Luise Drüke, *Senior European Affairs Officer, UNHCR, Brussels*

Gordon Fairweather, *Former Chairman, Immigration and Refugees Board of Canada*

Julio Féo, *Chairman, Consultores de Comunicacion y Direccion, Madrid*

Dennis Gallagher, *Executive Director, Refugee Policy Group, Washington*

John Gilbert, *Member of British Parliament*

Allan Gotlieb, *North American Deputy Chairman, Trilateral Commission; former Canadian Ambassador to the United States; former Deputy Minister of Immigration*

Jacques Groothaert, *Honorary Chairman, Générale de Banque, Brussels*

Barbara Harrell-Bond, *Founder and Director, Refugee Studies Programme, Oxford University*

Charles B. Heck, *North American Director, Trilateral Commission*

Neils Holm, *Chairman of the Board, Ramboll & Hannemann, Virum (Denmark)*

Gilbert Jaeger, *Chairman, Belgian Committee for Refugees, Brussels*

Soren Jessen-Petersen, *Director of Executive Office and External Affairs, United Nations High Commissioner for Refugees, Geneva*

Baron Daniel Janssen, *Chairman, Executive Committee, Solvay & Co., Brussels*

Reimut Jochimsen, *President, Central Bank of Northrhine-Westphalia, Düsseldorf*

André Juneau, *Executive Director, Immigration Policy, Employment & Immigration Canada*

Count Otto Lambsdorff, *European Chairman, Trilateral Commission; Member of the German Bundestag and Chairman of the Free Democratic Party; former Federal Minister of Economics*

Wenceslas de Lobkowicz, *Responsible for the Abolition of Border Controls on Persons, EC Commission, Brussels*

Winston Lord, *U.S. Assistant Secretary of State for East Asian and Pacific Affairs*

Roderick MacFarquhar, *Professor of Government and Director of the Fairbank Center for East Asian Research, Harvard University; former Member of British Parliament*

Philip L. Martin, *Professor of Agricultural Economics, University of California at Davis*

Jay Mazur, *President, International Ladies' Garment Workers' Union, New York*

Karen McBride, *Associate, Parliamentary Centre for Foreign Affairs and Foreign Trade, Ottawa*

Klaus Murmann, *Chairman, Federation of German Employers' Association, Cologne*

John Murray, *Secretary of the European Committee on Migration, Council of Europe, Strasbourg*

Makito Noda, *Senior Program Officer, Japan Center for International Exchange, Tokyo; Japanese Staff, Trilateral Commission*

Demetrios Papademetriou, *Senior Associate, Carnegie Endowment for International Peace; former Assistant Director for Immigration Policy and Research, Bureau of International Labor Affairs, U.S. Department of Labor*

Francisco Pinto Balsemao, *Former Prime Minister of Portugal*

Paul Révay, *European Director, Trilateral Commission, Paris*

Rozanne Ridgway, *Co-Chair, Atlantic Council of the United States; former U.S. Assistant Secretary of State for European and Canadian Affairs*

Michael Shenstone, *Special Advisor, Policy Planning Staff, External Affairs and International Trade Canada*

W.R. Smyser, *Adjunct Professor, Georgetown University; former Deputy UN High Commissioner for Refugees; former Director of Refugee Programs, U.S. Department of State*

Theo Sommer, *Editor in Chief, Die Zeit, Hamburg*

Myles Staunton, *Member of the Senate, Irish Republic*

Nick Swales, *Executive Assistant, Canadian Group of the Trilateral Commission*

Deborah Taylor, *Administrator, Canadian Group of the Trilateral Commission*

Michael Teitelbaum, *Program Officer, Alfred P. Sloan Foundation; Member, U.S. Commission on the Study of Migration and Cooperative Economic Development; Member, U.S. Commission on Immigration Reform*

Sir Charles Tidbury, *Member of the Board of Directors, Whitbread & Co., London*

Jerry Tinker, *Staff Director, Subcommittee on Immigration and Refugee Affairs, Judiciary Committee, U.S. Senate*

Ko-Yung Tung, *Chairman, Global Practice Group, O'Melveny & Myers, New York*

Jonas Widgren, *Coordinator, Intergovernmental Consultations on Migration, Refugees and Asylum Policies, Geneva*

Karen Hastie Williams, *Partner, Crowell & Moring, Washington*

Peter Witte, *Assistant to the North American Director, Trilateral Commission*

Otto Wolff von Amerongen, *Chairman, East Committee of German Industry, Cologne*

Warren Zimmermann, *Director, Refugee Programs Bureau, U.S. Department of State; former U.S. Ambassador to Yugoslavia*

Summary Highlights of
INTERNATIONAL MIGRATION CHALLENGES
IN A NEW ERA

Chapter II - Canada and the United States

"The long, rich tradition of immigration to Canada and the United States is one of the ultimate human manifestations of the upheavals of world history.... The proposition that membership in the society and opportunity for a better life can be provided to diverse peoples in exchange for hard work and democratic participation is a deeply held belief.... At the same time, immigration is a controversial, unsettled political question and a source of vigorous debate. Currently, that debate revolves around the broad question of whether sizeable immigration continues to enrich the economy and the culture or whether these nations, now mature and settled, need to substantially limit immigrant flows to secure prosperity and social cohesion among established populations." (p. 12)

Canada

"With a population of just over 27 million, Canada's annual target of 250,000 immigrants from 1992 to 1995...represents, at levels just under one percent of its population, sizeable flows...." (p. 17)

"Altogether, Canada's immigration policy has been steadily honed and adjusted to embody a workable balance between generosity and economic self-interest. This balance is the linchpin for the policy's political support and credibility...." (p. 22)

"Canada's effort to respond to the central migration development of the last decade—the political asylum crisis—has been both the most ambitious and the most successful in the world.... Canada has achieved what no other nation has been able to in the political asylum arena: it has a system that is timely and perceived to be fair. These are the twin characteristics that are required if nations are to both uphold international refugee standards and discourage unfounded claims." (pp. 23-24)

"A generous immigration program cannot be sustained unless integration is successful. Canada's approach to the task is its policy of multiculturalism.... Canada devotes an exceptional degree of attention to the complexity of the integration challenge." (pp. 24-26)

United States

"Always an ethnically mixed society, the United States is more so now than at any prior time. Net immigration, including illegal immigration, is about one million annually, with almost 90 percent from countries in Asia and the Americas." (p. 26)

Illegal Immigration "Despite the political importance of enacting employer sanctions (in 1986), their enforcement is not working well.... (T)he central flaw in the sanctions scheme that was enacted is the absence of requirements for secure identity documents.... The debate about illegal immigration is reviving because the United States has been unable to measurably limit illegal flows at a time of sluggish growth and broad-based economic restructuring. New solutions will require Americans to make trade-offs between the commitment to a generous but controlled immigration system and principles of individual freedom as they have been traditionally practiced and perceived." (pp. 31-32)

Refugee Policy "With the Cold War behind, refugee policy has lost its rationale and refugee admissions are increasingly anachronistic.... (P)olicy-makers seem quite comfortable with the status quo.... This, combined with the absence of an international strategic outlook that is enhaced by refugee resettlement, has produced stagnation in a policy arena where the U.S. has typically provided aggressive, high-minded leadership." (pp. 32-34)

Immigrant Integration "U.S. integration policy has been to rely on a healthy economy and the vitality of public institutions, such as the education system, to provide opportunity and training that brings newcomers into the mainstream of American life.... Disturbing signs are appearing...." (p. 35)

Regional Economic Integration "(R)educing migration pressures is regularly cited by all parties as one of the benefits of NAFTA.... Job-creating growth in migrant-sending countries lessens the need people feel to emigrate.... However, in the short-to-medium term,...economic development is also likely to stimulate migration pressures. And 'short-to-medium' in this connection is 10 to 20 years.... The realistic objective must be one of lessening the irregularity and unpredictability of illegal immigration, not of averting immigration completely." (pp. 37-38)

Chapter III - European Community Countries

"From 1850 to 1920, more than 50 million people, about 12 percent of Europe's total population, left.... Forty percent of the population of the British Isles left; and 30 percent left Italy and the Scandinavian countries.... (M)igrations were intrinsic to development and modernization processes, just as they are for many developing countries today." (p. 40)

"Today, Europe stands at the very crossroads of international migration pressures. It faces urgent demands from across the Oder-Neisse River to the east and the Mediterranean Sea to the south." (p. 40)

Europe and Immigration Today

The Foreigner Issue "Foreigners from outside the EC are concentrated in France and Germany, the two countries that most actively recruited guestworkers through programs that were considered temporary labor market measures. These two, with somewhat over one-third of the EC population, have two-thirds of the non-EC foreigner population. For both, Islamic immigrants are about one-third of their foreign populations and are seen to pose major dilemmas where immigrant integration issues are concerned." (pp. 41-43)

"Since the end of the guestworker programs, governments have declared that Europe is 'closed' to immigration from outside of Europe. However,...(t)he numbers that reside in Europe today as legacies of guestworker programs are higher than the number there when migrant workers were actively being recruited. This illustrates the power of immigrant networks as a dynamic of transnational processes. It further illustrates the substantial gap that has opened between political rhetoric and popular experience." (pp. 43-44)

East-West Pressures "As sobering as the economic projections are, it is humanitarian emergencies that represent the most dangerous migration scenario.... If ethnic conflict can be ameliorated, East-West movements should eventually be able to be regulated within acceptable bounds.... In addressing East-West migration pressures, EC countries are likely to pursue economic integration, steadily incorporating Eastern Europe into EC structures with their promise of political stability and economic improvement in the years ahead." (pp. 45-46)

South-North Pressures "More longstanding and more intractable than migration pressures from the East are those from the South.... Europe has no real choice but to commit itself to assistance efforts that narrow the widening prosperity gap with Mediterranean rim societies. This is likely to take the form of closer economic association, however, instead of the more comprehensive strategy of economic integration that is unfolding where East-West pressures are concerned." (pp. 46-47)

"The Mediterranean divide may not be a long-term one. With aggressive development efforts, the Maghreb, Egypt and Turkey could develop relatively quickly. The divide then would become the Sahara." (p. 48)

The Asylum Crisis "The most objectionable policy in the public mind is one where the nation appears unable to control a basic element of sovereignty, such as the choice of who resides in the country. This abdication of choice is what burgeoning asylum caseloads represent, and long-staying asylum populations symbolize national vulnerability." (p. 50)

"The nation with the biggest asylum burden (Germany) has now also taken the most sweeping, agonizing steps of any European nation to respond. Even so, changing laws and procedures for handling asylum cases, either in Germany or elsewhere in Europe, will not be enough. And politicians would be wise not to promise an end to the asylum problem. That is because asylum systems are bearing the burden not just of refugees and refugee-like people, but of migration pressures overall." (p. 52)

Immigration as an Issue of High Politics

"Europe sees immigration as inextricably bound up with its political, economic and social well-being, as well as its future security interests. This is very different from the way immigration is perceived and debated in Canada and the United States, at least at the present time." (p. 53)

Parties and Domestic Politics "Germany's experience has been the most painful, but it is symptomatic of Europe overall. The core difficulty is that Europe has become an immigration region, having neither planned nor chosen to be one. Leaders have been slow to grasp this new situation and its implications and have been unable or unwilling to take up questions regarding ways to regulate migration flows and manage cultural diversity. Even states that have accommodated substantial immigration, like France and Britain, steadfastly insist they are not immigration nations. Consequently, the policy debate that is needed about how immigration is changing European countries and the challenges that lie ahead has been occurring in the streets." (pp. 54-55)

"Unless European politics are able to bring the full complexity of migration questions into the open and propose and critique comprehensive solutions, the gap between politics and public experience will continue to widen. Closing that gap is a threshold requirement for political leaders to embrace.... Europe's collective efforts, through the European Community and other collaborative efforts, have begun to mobilize the kinds of responses and consensus that are needed to meet the challenge." (p. 55)

European Community Structures and Policy "European Community states are steadily ceding their national powers in this arena to European regional structures and cooperative mechanisms. This trend reflects a growing conviction at national levels that solutions to migration pressures must be found through international cooperation. It is a marked departure from just two or three years ago, when the habit was to rely on unilateral action, largely limited to entry controls." (p. 55)

"It remains to be seen how effective this extensive legal framework will be and how quickly European states will move to put it into actual practice.... Nevertheless, the many structures and policies that are evolving represent an impressive record of achievement. In combination, they constitute the principal elements of an immigration system. Nations' immigration systems consist of explicit practices and mechanisms to effect visa issuance; border controls; admission of immigrants and their family members and of refugees and asylum-seekers; workplace regulation; legal and naturalization rights of non-citizens; and expulsion procedures. The policies that govern these functions and the functions themselves are now all at varying stages of being established among European Community countries." (pp. 59-60)

Europe and Immigration Tomorrow

"The primary obstacle is the distance between European policy development processes on immigration questions and public opinion. As political leaders assert that Europe is not an immigration region, regional organizations have constructed a full-fledged immigration system." (p. 57)

A Closed Debate "Officials of member states have not invited broad consideration of measures that will have profound effects on daily life and about which public opinion must be better informed and more fully considered.... This closed policy-making style seriously jeopardizes the success of the entire enterprise, and contributes to Europe's democracy deficit." (p. 61)

The Plethora of Forums "The best evolution in this regard would be for the EC processes and institutions to become the primary European setting for immigration policy development and implementation. This would place immigration squarely into the framework where overarching issues of regional concern are handled. It would also overcome the deficiencies of the intergovernmental process.... In this connection, the Maastricht right of co-initiative should be fully utilized: the EC Commission should present an annual migration report to the European Parliament and Council that includes proposals for action. The presentation should be made by the Commissioner for Immigration and Asylum Issues, who would be Europe's de facto High Commissioner for Migrants. Furthermore, EC institutions should work closely and cooperatively with the United Nations High Commissioner for Refugees (UNHCR)." (p. 62)

Fortress Europe "Establishing immigration systems and policies in Europe should be the path to effective facilitation and regulation of migration flows that are inevitable and to incorporating immigration effectively into a nation's economic and social goals. Nevertheless, Fortress Europe could also be the outcome if policy implementation is not generous and is driven by xenophobia. Europe's response to refugees from ex-Yugoslavia represents a worrisome case.... Evidence that argues against the fear of a Fortress Europe is also strong...." (pp. 63-64)

"(S)hould the idea of a quota system take hold, levels of annual immigrant admissions could be proposed by the EC Commission, after consultation with the European Parliament, to the EC Council of Ministers. Or, the EC could establish a new position of High Commissioner for Immigration, with duties that would include making recommendations for meeting the EC's immigration needs.... A Migration Convention might also allow for a non-EC national legally residing in a member state to work in another EC country, thereby increasing the labor pool within the EC able to respond to the region's labor demands." (p. 65)

Chapter IV - Japan

"Japan's historical experience on migration matters is completely different from that of either North America or Europe.... However,... the picture is beginning to change." (p. 67)

Labor Shortages and Foreign Workers

"In 1992, Japan introduced a foreign worker trainee program intended to provide badly needed labor to certain Japanese employers while also giving training and experience to workers from less developed countries.... The intent is to train about 100,000 foreigners a year." (pp. 67-68)

The Demographic Imperative "Japan is at a crucial demographic and labor force crossroads which has profound...implications." (p. 68)

Illegal Workers "The employment of illegal workers has...sharply risen, particularly in blue-collar and low-level service jobs. Estimates of the size of the illegal population show steady increases, from 160,000 in 1991 to 278,000 by mid-1992. This is a dramatic increase...over a few tens of thousands just three years ago.... The same issues and problems that have become familiar dilemmas in other advanced industrial societies are now arising in Japan." (pp. 69-70)

Government Policy "Because the law prohibits admission of unskilled workers, the government's foreign worker program has been explained not as a guestworker program but as an effort to achieve training and development goals for labor-source countries.... Nomenclature notwithstanding, Japan's steps towards adopting the guestworker model to confront its demographic destiny have all the earmarks of the European experience of the 1960s and '70s." (pp. 71-72)

"Introducing foreign labor without systematically preparing the public for the significant consequences it may have for Japanese life could invite serious social and cultural antagonisms. On the other hand, Japan may be able to contain the broader social effects of guestworker programs by carefully segregating work among Japanese and foreigners and by imposing tight limits...on the latitude given to foreign workers while in Japan. Albeit limited in scope, the journey on which Japan seems to be embarked presents the developed world with one of the more remarkable migration policy experiments underway in any Trilateral country today." (pp. 72-73)

Japan's International Role

"Japan has become increasingly active and engaged in some aspects of the international refugee agenda. It has defined its role as primarily one of providing financial support for humanitarian activities.... (I)t may not be possible for Japan to limit its role to 'checkbook diplomacy'." (p. 73)

Chapter V - The International Community and Refugees:
Different Contexts, Changing Approaches

"The end of the Cold War has ushered in a fourth period.... Generous refugee resettlement by third countries is no longer politically attractive nor consistent with broader strategic objectives, so humanitarian relief has begun to concentrate on care-in-place and be accompanied by political initiatives to defuse the conflicts themselves." (pp. 75-76)

The Aftermath of the Gulf War

"For the first time, the consequences of a refugee crisis were designated a political threat that called for political countermeasures. The international community had taken the unprecedented act of authorizing humanitarian intervention.... A (UNHCR) mission calling for protection to be provided *within* the country in which the refugee is in danger was entirely new.... Ultimately, the authority for UNHCR's work in Iraq was based not on (Security Council) Resolution 688, but on a separate Memorandum of Understanding negotiated with Iraqi authorities precisely to resolve the contradiction between UNHCR's mandate and the special circumstances of the Iraqi case.... Safety zones can be a pragmatic alternative to first asylum, but they cannot be established without the acquiescence of state authorities, if they are to be viable from a protection standpoint." (pp. 76-77)

Cambodia

"The Cambodia (repatriation) operation...is inextricably linked with the most intense, comprehensive effort being made to date to facilitate peace in a deeply damaged country. As such, repatriation is an integral part of the peace process and an important test of the role humanitarian initiatives can play in achieving bold, new political objectives." (p. 78)

"How far does UNHCR's responsibility extend once refugees return home?...Institutional and policy links between repatriation and re-integration/development activities must be effectively made if repatriation is to break the cycle of turmoil that leads to further refugee flight." (pp. 79-81)

Ex-Yugoslavia

"UNHCR's dilemma has been deepened by the need for military protection to enable it to protect and deliver relief supplies. This represents an historic departure for agencies whose effectiveness is anchored in a fierce devotion to neutrality and impartiality, so as to be able to work on all sides of political conflicts with strictly humanitarian aims as the objective. In contrast, the Security Council and its forces have distinctly political purposes. The danger is that linking these military forces to UNHCR's humanitarian duties could jeopardize and taint UNHCR's ability to operate with confidence among all relevant parties.

Nevertheless, conditions on the ground dictated the outcome. Humanitarian assistance could not be delivered in the absence of security. The linkage between humanitarian aid and military cover had to be made." (p. 82)

"In the eyes of UNHCR, its work in ex-Yugoslavia brings it into a symbiotic relationship with political processes dedicated to finding peaceful solutions to the conflict.... By containing displacement, it sees its humanitarian activity as making time and space available for political initiatives to bear fruit.... Albeit courageous and perhaps visionary, humanitarianism has proven to be no match for deadly aggression." (p. 83)

"Moreover, ex-Yugoslavia demonstrates that efforts to concentrate on the country of origin can also become a way to bottle up genuine refugees in their own country, rationalizing that they do not require asylum in other places because humanitarian agencies have been dispatched to the source. This is a dangerous tendency inherent in country-of-origin strategies, important and urgent though they are. The offer of asylum and temporary refuge must always be available as a genuine option for refugee emergencies. Relief agencies should not be required to operate in a milieu of life-threatening conditions combined with closed borders." (p. 85)

Haiti

"The importance being attached to Haiti by the new Administration demonstrates how differently security and national interests may begin to look in a post-Cold War setting. Nations like Haiti, that have not been of any strategic interest to major Trilateral powers, except to be kept non-Communist, are beginning to demand attention because their poverty and oppression generates instability that can spark sizeable migrations. Such emergency, unregulated migrations can, in turn, undermine the well-being of neighboring states." (p. 87)

Chapter VI - Where Do We Go From Here?:
A Framework for Policy

"The causes of contemporary migrations are deeply embedded in the social, economic and political conditions of our times. Yet to the extent that nations have migration policies at all, most handle them as narrow, particularistic functions. To be effective, policy must go beyond conventional control and humanitarian measures, so that managing migration pressures becomes part of nations' central economic, political and security objectives.

Comprehensive policies that address the causes of political and economic migrations will require a fundamental shift in the outlook and actions of Trilateral states. That shift should be anchored in a new international imperative, the right of individuals to stay where they are. Most international migration is an act of desperation, not choice. The vast majority of individuals prefer home and will stay there, if conditions are even barely tolerable. It is that impulse that policy must build on." (p. 89)

Table of Contents

List of Tables and Figures

I. WHO ARE TODAY'S MIGRANTS? WHY ARE THEY ON THE MOVE?

Migration is as old as human history and as new as the forces shaping events in a post-Cold War world. Through the ages, it has functioned as a primary source of human progress that has largely been a positive force for individuals and civilizations. In modern times, migration has been fundamentally an outgrowth of the agricultural revolution and urbanization. At the same time, contemporary migrations are also increasingly generated by wars, human rights deprivations and poverty.

The vast majority of migrants move within their own countries, the next-largest share move across national boundaries within the less-developed world, and a relatively small share cross borders to developed countries. Although proportionately small, the numbers coming to the developed world are sizeable and growing. Because many of today's migrants were not properly admitted or are distinct in racial, ethnic or religious terms from host societies, there is a perception in some receiving societies, particularly in Europe, that the nation has lost control over its destiny. This has led to fierce political debate and to calls for dramatic policy changes.

In the international arena, greater migration flows and emergency mass movements, whether or not they actually bring people to Trilateral and other advanced industrial nations, are occurring during a period of massive historical transition. With the end of the Cold War, we are moving from one international age to a new, as yet undefined era. Some prophesy that our times portend changes as profound as those that followed the French and Bolshevik revolutions.[1]

What is certain is that the changes are unleashing powerful processes of social and political fragmentation at the same time that nations are increasingly interdependent from an economic and security standpoint. With growing migration pressures occurring in this time of extraordinary change and uncertainty, large numbers on the move can be the source of political instability and dangerous upheavals. International migration is emerging as a critical concern, therefore, for peace and stability in a new age.

A. ANATOMY OF THE ISSUES

The nations of the New World have traditionally been immigrant-receiving societies. Thus, Canada and the United States, for example, were created and settled by Europeans, who came in especially large numbers during the last decades of the 19th century up to World War I. European Community countries and Japan have not historically been immigrant nations. Nevertheless, during recent decades Europe steadily began to be home to substantial and growing numbers of foreigners. For nations bound by assumptions of shared ethnicity or nationality, immigration is seen as a fundamental threat to identity and national unity. In Japan and elsewhere in East Asia, the issues are generally not on the political agenda at this time. However, the specter of China and its future political and economic course poses a major geopolitical question within the region and globally that could have an important migration dimension.

Although European and most other states do not define themselves as immigration nations, traditional definitions of migrant sending and receiving countries have broken down dramatically. More and more, nations with no migration tradition find themselves confronted with migration questions, and others that were strictly sending or receiving states are experiencing the opposite or both phenomena. Consider these situations:

- Italy and Spain, which supplied workers in large numbers to northern neighbors just ten years ago, now host growing numbers of migrants from northern Africa and Eastern Europe.

- Hungary, a source of refugees throughout the Cold War, moved quickly after the fall of the Berlin Wall to be accepted as a state that adheres to the United Nations Convention on Refugees. It now provides asylum to victims of ex-Yugoslavia's civil war and is seen by Romanians as a source of jobs and opportunity.

- Poland—from which large numbers of seasonal workers go to Germany, France and Austria—worries about the brisk traffic of traders and criminal elements from the former Soviet Union.

- The growing movement of Guatemalans and Salvadorans into Mexico has led it to patrol its southern border while hundreds of thousands of Mexicans continue to cross the U.S. border illegally each year.

- One-third of Canada's political asylum caseload is applicants from third countries who have entered Canada from the United States.

- Russia, whose Jewish population is emigrating to Israel and the

United States in massive numbers and whose elites sought to leave throughout the Cold War, hosts a sizeable population of Armenian refugees. Many more groups are beginning to seek its protection, as conditions in numerous trouble spots on its periphery continue to deteriorate.

These and similar examples raise basic questions. Who are today's migrants? Why are they on the move?

1. Legally Admitted Residents (immigrants) and Non-Residents (non-immigrants)

For immigrant-receiving nations, the 1980s have been a period of historically high immigration levels that promise to continue and increase through the 1990s. Just under 9 million newcomers came to the United States in the 1980s,[2] for example, more than in 1901-1910, the highest previous immigration decade.

In addition, the numbers of non-residents have grown dramatically in all industrialized nations. Foreign students, technically trained personnel, multinational corporation executives and managers, scientists and experts in a wide variety of fields in which global enterprises and markets exist now comprise a growing international elite. They come from nearly every nation, move frequently and freely, and are not generally viewed as a policy or migration control problem.

2. Contract Labor Migrants

Policies similar to Europe's guestworker schemes of the 1950s and '60s are widespread. In particular, many countries in the Middle East rely on foreign workers from labor surplus countries nearby and in South and East Asia. Contract labor arrangements exist in many parts of Asia and between Asian nations and nations in other regions of the world. A number of these governments, for example Pakistan and the Philippines, actively promote emigration of their nationals.

The instability inherent in contract labor arrangements was vividly illustrated at the outbreak of the Gulf War when almost two million workers poured out of Kuwait, Iraq and Saudi Arabia, forced to return to nations already unable to provide jobs and further burdened by the loss of substantial remittance payments that expatriate workers supplied. In addition, women now comprise a substantial proportion of the contract labor population. They are particularly vulnerable to exploitative situations. Nonetheless, contract labor arrangements are widely seen to be mutually beneficial from an employment and economic standpoint. They are likely to continue to be prevalent, particularly in Asia and in countries that are not liberal democracies.

3. Illegal Immigrants

Virtually every industrialized nation now houses populations of illegal immigrants. Some slip across borders. Others overstay the terms of authorized visas or travel documents, originally issued for tourist, study or temporary work purposes. Most plan only temporary or episodic stays. But for a high proportion and for a variety of reasons, their sojourn becomes long-term.

Illegals generally work in marginal or undesirable jobs. By and large, they do not directly displace large numbers of native workers at the outset, but contribute to circumstances that undermine overall working conditions and impede labor market adjustments over the longer term.

4. Asylum-Seekers

Non-citizens within a country who apply to the host government for political asylum according to the terms of the international refugee convention are known as asylum-seekers. Political asylum was an exceptional event before the 1980s. It typically arose in the case of defectors. Beginning in the early '80s, caseloads in all industrialized nations, except Japan, ballooned.

Although some asylum applications are clear attempts at subterfuge (adjudication is protracted, often taking years, and applicants have varying degrees of work privileges or access to social services while waiting), most asylum-seekers come from countries and circumstances where a mixture of economic hardship and political chaos prevails. As a result, despite low approval rates in most countries, those whose applications are denied are frequently never returned to their home countries. The asylum-seeker may not be a refugee under the provisions of international refugee law, but most nations are unwilling, for humanitarian and domestic political reasons, to return people to nations like Lebanon, Liberia, Somalia, or Sri Lanka.

Asylum-seekers are by far the most controversial category of international migrants in industrialized nations and arguably the most difficult migration situation today to address.

5. Refugees

In 1970, there were 2.5 million refugees in the care of the international assistance community. Today, the number exceeds 17.5 million (see Appendix A). An equal number are displaced within national borders.[3] In international law, refugees are persons with a fear of persecution based on "race, religion, national origin, political opinion or membership in a social group."

Today's refugees are overwhelmingly in the less developed world (the 20 countries hosting the highest numbers have average per capita incomes of $700), and they are the victims of war and civil strife, particularly protracted Cold War conflicts. Less than one percent have any chance of resettlement in the West because sizeable resettlement programs are no longer being mounted, except for those with family or other ties. The majority who are outside their countries live in camps administered by the United Nations (UN) and other non-governmental agencies. This international humanitarian aid system has received growing levels of resources but remains chronically understaffed and inadequately funded in the face of mounting demands and unimagined humanitarian emergencies like that in ex-Yugoslavia.

Although there are significant, provocative issues associated with each of these groups, it is the latter three categories—illegal immigrants, asylum-seekers and refugees—around which the migration debate in the industrialized world largely revolves. The end of the Cold War has placed a spotlight on the dilemmas posed by open borders within Europe and the virulence of ethnic hatred in the Balkans. However, the forces underlying contemporary migrations substantially predate the parting of the Iron Curtain and are rooted in conditions of life that propel people to move.

B. CAUSES OF CONTEMPORARY MIGRATIONS

In broad terms, people on the move are either primarily economic or political migrants. Thus, contract labor and illegal immigrants are economic migrants; asylum-seekers and refugees are political migrants; and legally admitted residents include both economic and political migrants, depending on a nation's immigration policy. Although categories of migrants are distinct in law and policy, related conditions, singly and in combination, have generated the flows.

1. Wars, Strife, and Human Rights Failures

The 1970s and '80s were marked by protracted war and civil strife in many countries and regions of the world. Some of the conflicts, such as those in Southeast Asia, southern Africa and Central America, were fueled and escalated by U.S.-Soviet antagonisms. Ninety percent of the casualties in these proxy wars have been civilians.[4] Furthermore, increasingly sophisticated and plentiful weaponry has caused devastating injuries for large numbers of innocent victims. Nor do injuries end when the fighting stops. As they try to rebuild, repatriated refugees and residents face the continuing danger of land mines that regularly claim lives and limbs in countries like Afghanistan, Cambodia and Mozambique.

The peril to non-combatants as well as the duration and devastation of the proxy and other wars have caused massive population displacements. Depending on the international politics of the situation, the victims were seen to be refugees (Cambodia, Vietnam, Afghanistan), asylum-seekers (Ethiopia, Nicaragua, Sri Lanka) or illegal immigrants (El Salvador, Somalia, Guatemala).

Both greater democratization and the resurgence of repressed nationality conflicts are the political processes that have been unleashed by the end of the Cold War. Both also carry within them the seeds of refugee movements. If fledgling democracies falter, authoritarian regimes could again reappear, sparking social and political conflicts that could generate refugee flows. More immediate and probably more dangerous are ethnic conflicts, as the dissolution of Bosnia demonstrates, that escalate and result in warfare.[5] Already, there are more wars underway than at any time in modern history. In the case of ex-Yugoslavia, the war is particularly diabolical in that refugees are not simply the byproduct of aggression but its object: the very purpose of ethnic cleansing as a military objective is to create refugees.

Communally based violence is likely to deepen in parts of Eastern Europe and the former Soviet Union (FSU), where long-standing enmities have been repressed for decades and where ethnic identity is now being used as an ideology to interpret history. Ethnic warfare will also almost certainly increase in the developing world, replacing guerrilla wars of national liberation. Because of cheap, accessible modern weaponry, civil wars devastate the limited progress that may have been made in building infrastructure in poor countries and can displace very large numbers of people, because of population size and density.[6]

Sometimes actual or potential refugee crises are solvable if the victimized population has a homeland elsewhere. Ethnic Germans in

Poland and parts of the FSU, for example, have steadily been returning to Germany, even though it was generations ago that their forefathers were relocated. Similarly, Greeks from areas in Central Asia have been returning to Greece, and Russians living in the Baltic states and Central Asia have begun returning to Russia. Such population "unmixing" can be a pragmatic solution to minority problems. Modern history even includes examples of formal population exchanges in quest of peaceful relations among groups. However, the more likely future trend is cases like ex-Yugoslavia, where populations are ethnically mixed, antagonistic, and lacking any options for relocation to solve their problems.[7]

2. Economic Development and Population Patterns

Many of the development gains of the 1960s and '70s slowed or were reversed in the 1980s, due to war, recession, and debt. With the major exception of much of East Asia, job creation and improvements in living standards lagged seriously at a time when high 1950s and '60s birth rates poured unprecedented numbers of new workers into labor markets. Where cross-national linkages existed, either through longstanding labor market relationships (such as those between Mexico and the United States), or historic ties (such as between northern Africa and Europe), South-North migration accelerated.

In addition, export-led development strategies that have prevailed in many countries, particularly in Asia, together with overpopulation, poverty, or unemployment, seem to induce emigration. As a leading source of investment capital, even Japan is no longer impervious. The same is, of course, true for the United States and other nations. Major investment flows seem to be correlated with certain forms of migration in a reverse flow.[8]

All available evidence suggests that migration pressures as a consequence of global inequality will only mount. The world is increasingly a place with a declining proportion of rich people and a growing proportion of poor people.

A distinguished demographer calls recent demographic trends "revolutionary, a virtual discontinuity with all human history." It took from the appearance of the species until 1800 for world population to reach one billion human beings. It took until 1987 to reach five billion. We are now adding an additional billion each decade, although annual percentage increases have dropped slightly from just over two percent in the 1960s to about 1.7 percent. Most of the growth in world population has taken place in the last 40 years. By 2025, world population is likely to exceed eight billion, with 95 percent of the increase having occurred in less developed nations. The growth of this "external proletariat," as Arnold Toynbee termed it, is most rapid in Africa, followed by South Asia and Latin America. Population growth is considerably slower in Western Europe and Japan.[9] With these demographic trends comes strong momentum for continued growth, populations with high proportions of children who will continue to enter labor markets in huge numbers, and runaway urbanization. This profile produces international migrants, who now come from many (though not all) rapid-growth nations.[10]

A crucial question is how a rich world of stable population size can interact with a less developed world of dramatic population growth. The task is enormous. By 2010, about 730 million persons will have been added to the working-age population in the developing world. During the period of the most robust job growth in the United States in the 1980s, to provide a comparison, the economy produced two million new jobs annually. The need to generate jobs is unprecedented. However, even with vastly accelerated economic growth, the rate of population growth in much of the less developed world is likely to overwhelm any gains in employment opportunities that might be made.

Another illustration of the scale of what is ahead comes from information about migrant remittances. Foreign exchange generated by remittances is estimated to have been $71 billion in 1991, a number second only to oil sales, whereas official development assistance stands at about $51 billion.[11] Officially tallied remittances come largely through contract labor programs. The actual figure, because of sizeable informal flows that have not been measured, is far higher. Thus, international migration is a critical factor in sustaining many nations' economies.

3. International Connections

International migration flows are not random. They track close connections that have been established, often decades ago, between and among nations. These connections are rooted in colonialism, war and military occupation, labor recruitment, and economic interaction. Examples of the forms these connections take are as follows:

- Indians move to Britain and Canada, their Commonwealth partners.
- Korean war brides led the way for today's sizeable Korea-U.S. flow.

- Turkish guestworkers in Germany sent for family members instead of returning to them at home.
- Cuban elites, who identified with capitalism and whose wealth derived from American investment, fled to Miami after the 1959 revolution.

Once migration footholds are established, family members join successful migrants, remittances link communities across great distances, and established immigrant groups help the newly arrived find work and negotiate seemingly alien ways and places. Migration itself then becomes a new connection between nations, evolving into a social process that is increasingly sustained by factors that are largely beyond the realm of government action or the economic impulses that originally generated it.

Colonialism and military occupation may be outdated forms, but new, analogous transnational linkages are being created as economic interdependence deepens. These linkages are giving rise to many new forms and sources of migration. Combined with inexpensive international transportation and communications systems that bring information and images of far-distant places to the most remote villages on earth, both the means and knowledge that are required to move are broadly available.

4. Receptivity to Migrants in Advanced Industrial Nations

A complex set of supply/demand interactions must exist for migration pressures to become actual flows. And the demand element of the equation is frequently overlooked or not adequately acknowledged. For many advanced industrial societies, their history, their values, and the structure of their economies make them receptive to immigration, public opinion notwithstanding.

The belief systems that undergird most democratic systems rest upon a set of humanitarian and social values that are the basis for admitting refugees and family members of earlier immigrants. For many nations in Western Europe, for example, guestworker recruitment ceased in the early 1970s. However, there are sizeable populations of newcomers 20 years later because guestworkers are permitted to have family members join them where they live and work. The idea that a person would be denied the right to have family members with him if his stay is for long periods is simply unacceptable in many nations.

Similarly, U.S. immigration is disproportionately dominated by family reunion admissions. This leads to a phenomenon known as "chain migration," wherein the admission of one person can, through the legitimate entry of relatives, generate a significant number of additional immigrants. The ripple effect would largely disappear if the law limited immigration to members of the nuclear family, cutting off the admission of married adult siblings of immigrants. Proposals along these lines have been debated by the Congress but have always been soundly defeated as a violation of basic precepts of equity and historical fairness. This is because the change would curtail the immigration rights of currently immigrating groups, among them Asians, whose admission was barred on racial grounds until the 1960s.

Due-process-based legal systems are another manifestation of democratic values that frustrate tight immigration controls. The asylum crisis both in Europe and North America is, in fact, a paralysis of decision-making systems not equipped to adjudicate large numbers of cases rapidly, when the stakes can be life or death for an individual.

Nor are many countries particularly comfortable deporting individuals to places that are dangerous and impoverished, even if refugee status is not granted. The approval rate for asylum applicants in Europe is only about five percent. However, the large majority of those denied are still not removed, often for humanitarian and public image reasons. This reluctance extends to other methods of control. In the United States, identification systems to check unlawful employment of migrants are widely seen to be a hallmark of the police state.

Demand is also a function of the economies of developed nations. International trade and markets have restructured developed country economies in ways that expand the supply of low-wage jobs, especially in major cities. Traditional manufacturing jobs have diminished, often replaced with lower paid, less skilled production jobs, and service sectors have grown very rapidly, creating substantial numbers of new, low-wage jobs. Immigrants are more likely than indigenous workers to take these jobs, a trend that is not likely to change as low rates of population growth and aging become more marked in many advanced societies.

Although regulated, sometimes generous, levels of immigration can make important contributions to the economic health of developed countries, migration is not the answer for the job-creation challenge in less developed countries. Under any realistic scenario, immigration opportunities in advanced industrial societies will remain modest when viewed against the employment needs of the rest of the world.

*   *   *

International migration is a structural characteristic of broad social, economic and political themes in today's world. The dilemma posed by international migration pressures will not solve itself. It requires concerted efforts and new priorities by individual nations and the international community.

II. Canada and the United States

Tip O'Neill, the venerable Boston politician who occupied one of the most powerful positions in U.S. political life, liked to observe that "all politics are local." His adage captures the singular personality of immigrant nations.

The long, rich tradition of immigration to Canada and the United States is one of the ultimate human manifestations of the upheavals of world history. The mosaic of immigrants' lives planted that history by bits and pieces in countrysides and communities throughout Canada and the United States. Thus, the nationhood that has grown from the immigrant experience is one uniquely based on loyalty to a collection of democratic values and civic virtues, rather than to ethnic, nationality, or religious bonds.

With the exception of indigenous groups and of African slaves, whose immigration was forced, Canada and the United States were peopled by groups who chose to make new lives in new lands. Immigration has been and continues to be a source of nation-building. The ethnic and religious diversity that characterizes these societies is viewed as a positive value and a source of national strength. The proposition that membership in the society and opportunity for a better life can be provided to diverse peoples in exchange for hard work and democratic participation is a deeply held belief that successive generations fight to perpetuate and perfect.

At the same time, immigration is a controversial, unsettled political question and a source of vigorous debate. Currently, that debate revolves around the broad question of whether sizeable immigration continues to enrich the economy and the culture or whether these nations, now mature and settled, need to substantially limit immigrant flows to secure prosperity and social cohesion among established populations. The question is recurring and the debate revolves around established legal instruments and administrative practices that together constitute these nations' immigration policies.

A. WHAT CONSTITUTES IMMIGRATION POLICY?

The immigration policies of Canada and the United States are articulated in national laws and implemented by executive agencies charged with their administration. Canada has a minister for immigration affairs with Cabinet rank, who directs the work of a ministry called Immigration and Employment Canada. Immigration concerns receive high-level consideration in overall government deliberations on domestic and foreign policy as a result. The United States handles immigration questions at the sub-Cabinet level. Immigration functions that must be carried out within the borders of the country are the responsibility of a bureau within the justice ministry; those carried out abroad are the responsibility of consular officials, whose work is guided by a bureau within the foreign ministry. This structure produces less comprehensive policymaking and cohesion in responding to new immigration developments and more control by the legislative branch.

Regardless of the organizational approach, immigration policy addresses three basic questions: Who? How many? From where?

1. Who?
Immigration policy seeks to admit people for social, humanitarian and economic reasons.

Social objectives are met by the admission of relatives of immigrants. Family unity has and continues to be the cornerstone of immigration policy for Canada and the United States. Which family members should be defined as "relatives" for purposes of immigration eligibility is a subject of continuing debate. Traditions in the receiving society favor definitions limited to the nuclear family—parents and unmarried children and siblings—whereas immigrant groups press for broadened definitions that include extended family members—grandparents and married siblings and children.

A second point of debate about generous family unity policies is a concern that family immigrants take rather than contribute economically. Family-based immigration is alleged to be an inefficient means of selecting workers that contributes to a decline in the skill levels of the workforce.

Much of this argument misjudges the character of family-based immigration. Family-connection immigrants are also workers. Immigrants are typically admitted under family reunification provisions who could also qualify in virtually all professional and technical occupations specified in immigration laws. Indirectly, family reunification also admits workers with skills.

More important, however, is the economic and social role the family plays in immigrant adaptation. Families ease the considerable social and cultural dislocations caused by immigration and, by serving as intermediaries to the host society, enable the newcomer to adapt. Family and household structures are also primary factors in promoting high economic achievement. They are crucial resources in the formation of immigrant businesses, which often revitalize urban neighborhoods and specialized economic sectors. These successful social and economic transitions lay the foundations that are needed if the children of immigrants are to be effective citizen-workers of the next generation.[12]

Humanitarian objectives are met through refugee resettlement and assistance programs. These programs frequently involve very large numbers of people in response to international emergencies, such as the 1979 Southeast Asian boat crisis. In one year, the United States admitted more that 140,000 people from emergency camps in the region, for example.

Through resettlement programs that have, in some cases, spanned decades, up to ten percent or more of the populations of countries like Cuba now live in the United States. These programs resettled hundreds of thousands of individuals because they fled Communist regimes, to which any realistic hope of timely return was precluded. At the same time, generous refugee admissions programs for the victims of Communism, who were hailed as heroes, was consistent with and served the larger geopolitical objectives of the West. With the end of the Cold War, the political rationale for such efforts has disappeared and a new paradigm has not yet replaced it.

Instead, the emergence of burgeoning political asylum caseloads has dominated the refugee debate in the 1980s, posing thorny new questions about how to carry out the humanitarian objectives of immigration policy in circumstances where intending refugees self-select and enter the country, rather than being designated abroad and then brought to the country.

Economic objectives, always a feature of immigration policy, have increasingly become a driving force in immigration policy-making. Through differing selection mechanisms, both Canada and the United States have recently legislated increases in immigration levels by significantly expanding immigration opportunities for people with sought-after skills.

The labor market dimensions of immigration and its place in the economic future of these societies signal a response to fundamental currents of history and global economic interdependence.

In practice, connections between prospective immigrants and employers generally occur before the applicant passes through the formal steps of immigrating. This happens in several ways. Many enter the country illegally, find work, and employers petition for them to be admitted. Others who are in the country with temporary visas (such as foreign students, for example) become associated with particular employers through training or post-graduate learning programs.

Thus, immigration for economic purposes is frequently not a beginning but an intermediary step in a process of labor market responses originating in non-immigrant policies. A significant share of immigrants have had experience in the country and have made a substantial connection to some part of the society or economy which is then ratified by formal immigration processes, as compared to the government or employers selecting immigrants from a pool waiting abroad.

2. How Many?

For more than a century, numerical limits to annual immigration flows have been imposed in Canada and the United States. For Canada, establishing those limits was for some time a distinct element of population policy goals that sought settlement of sparsely inhabited regions in its western provinces.

More recently, Canada introduced careful proportionality among its family, refugee, and labor market immigration streams. The labor market stream is further calibrated by regulating the proportion of workers that are admitted for any particular occupation to prevent occupations from becoming immigrant-saturated. In this way, native Canadians are not disadvantaged by immigrants in labor markets. Such mechanisms offer ways of handling the "how many?" question.

The United States has not consciously sought to make policy connections between its immigration levels and other national objectives. Its system is widely known as the quota system for admitting immigrants. Indeed, quotas, or numerical ceilings, do govern the admission of various categories of immigrants. But the ceilings have been highly arbitrary. They are established by the Congress as a measure of what the political traffic will bear, given the pleadings of employer representatives and ethnic communities who want immigration policy to favor their needs. Inadvertently, therefore, but still significantly, immigration is now a primary source of population growth, a trend that is slowing the rate at which U.S. society is ageing.

Observers often theorize that immigration levels should reflect some calculus of a nation's absorptive capacity. Because immigrants cluster in particular communities or regions, facilities (such as housing) and services (such as education) can become severely strained from high immigration levels.

Although there are exceptions, absorptive capacity is more psychology than science. If a people feels affinity, loyalty, or historical purpose with particular immigrant groups, very large numbers can be successfully integrated, objective measures of absorptive capacity notwithstanding. Cases in point are the departure of Jews since 1989 from the Soviet Union to Israel and the exodus of ethnic Germans from occupied lands in the East to modern Germany.

The opposite is also true. Relatively modest numbers can become seemingly indigestible knots in societies that are unable to open up social and economic mobility structures to people with different traditions and values. Such is the case with certain Muslim populations in parts of Europe.

3. From Where?

Until 1965, the United States based the geographical distribution of immigration source countries upon a formula that mirrored the national origins of its population. Not only did this system dramatically favor Europeans, it also explicitly barred Asians from immigrating. Through different mechanisms but with similar results, Canada pursued a "whites only" immigration policy until the late 1960s.

Today, these laws are viewed as anachronistic, having been replaced with laws based on country-of-origin neutrality. Immigration to Canada and the United States is dominated by Asians and Latin Americans because (a) family-unity-based selection priorities automatically favor newer immigrant groups; and (b) demand for immigration has shifted, arising, by and large, from the less developed regions of the world.

Still, established populations are habitually anxious about the dominance of unfamiliar, new groups among immigrant populations. In the United States "diversity visas" have been added to current law, for example. These are slots specifically designated to go to countries that are underrepresented in current immigration streams. Seemingly innocuous, such provisions are not dissimilar in practice from national origin preferences. They illustrate the overwhelming tendency of populations to try to reproduce, rather than transform themselves. Because immigration is a transforming phenomenon, the answers to the questions of who, how many, and from where have profound implications.

While Canadian and U.S. immigration traditions and patterns have many shared characteristics, these two nations are distinct and approach the same enterprise in often rather different ways.

B. CANADA

A nation founded by two nations, Canada today is home not only to the descendants of French and British settlers but also to people from many other countries. After World War I, relatively low levels of immigration persisted until the 1960s. Numbers climbed steadily until 1982, when the government made sharp reductions because of economic decline. In 1985, the government again decided upon steady increases.

Canada now has five-year immigration planning cycles within which immigration levels are reviewed and adjusted annually. The planning levels are goals (which are usually not precisely achieved in practice), not quotas or ceilings. From 1989 to 1991, Canada increased its immigration by almost 20 percent (162,000 to 205,000). With a population of just over 27 million, Canada's annual target of 250,000 immigrants from 1992 to 1995 (see Table 1) represents, at levels just under one percent of its population, sizeable flows that are intended to achieve a significantly larger population by 2000.

Although federal and provincial jurisdiction over immigration is concurrent in Canada, Quebec is the only province that has exercised the option to determine its own policy.[13] For Quebec, immigration represents a means for it to increase its number of French-speaking citizens.[14] For the rest of Canada, the Immigration Minister sets admissions targets in consultation with provincial officials, whose interests turn primarily on the impact immigrants have on the services and social programs they administer. The result is that long-range national goals are sometimes modified to address provinces' concerns.

Canada's parliamentary system gives the Immigration Minister considerable flexibility to adjust regulations, annual targets and other critical elements of policy execution. This allows for a system that can

TABLE 1
The Canadian Immigration Plan, 1991 to 1995
(planned immigration levels by planning component)

	1990*	1991	1992	1993	1994	1995
Family Class	72,500	80,000	95,000	95,000	85,000	85,000
Refugees						
government-assisted refugees and members of designated classes (selected abroad)	13,000	13,000	13,000	13,000	13,000	13,000
privately sponsored refugees and members of designated classes (selected abroad)	24,000	23,500	17,000	20,000	15,000	15,000
refugees landed in Canada (after 1/1/89)	5,000	10,000	20,000	25,000	25,000	25,000
Independent Immigrants						
principal applicants	25,500	20,000	21,500	22,500	29,000	29,000
spouses and other accompanying dependents	25,000	21,000	20,000	25,000	33,000	33,000
Assisted Relatives						
principal applicants	7,000	7,000	9,000	8,500	11,500	11,500
spouses and other accompanying dependents	11,000	12,500	16,500	15,000	19,000	19,000
Business Immigrants						
principal applicants	5,000	7,000	7,000	6,500	5,000	5,000
spouses and other accompanying dependents	13,500	21,000	21,000	19,500	14,500	14,500
Retirees	4,000	5,000	5,000	0	0	0
TOTAL	**200,000**	**220,000**	**250,000**	**250,000**	**250,000**	**250,000**

Source: Employment and Immigration Canada, *Annual Report to Parliament: Immigration Plan for 1991-95*, 1990

* The 1990 numbers are estimates prepared in June 1990.

TABLE 2
**Canadian Selection Criteria
(The "Points System")***

Factor	Units of Assessment	Notes
Education	12 maximum	
Specific Vocational Preparation	15 maximum	
Experience	8 maximum	0 units is an *automatic processing bar* unless (i) applicant has arranged employment and (ii) employer accepts lack of experience.
Occupation	10 maximum	0 units is an *automatic processing bar* unless applicant has arranged employment.
Arranged Employment	10	
Age	10 maximum	10 units if 21 to 44; 2 units deducted for each year under 21 or over 44
Knowledge of Official Language(s)	15 maximum	
Personal Suitability	10 maximum	
Levels Control	10 maximum	
TOTAL	**100**	
PASS MARK	**70**	
Bonus for all Assisted Relatives	10 (60 pass mark)	if application is accompanied by an undertaking of assistance
Additional Bonus for these Assisted Relatives: married sons and daughters, brothers and sisters	5 (55 pass mark)	

Source: Employment and Immigration Canada, *Annual Report to Parliament: Immigration Plan for 1991-95*, 1990

* The Quebec selection system has some differences in the factors and the units of assessment, but the intent and results are similar.

be quite responsive to changes in labor markets, international events, and public opinion.

1. Profile of the System

The major elements of Canada's immigration system are set forth in the Immigration Act of 1967, as amended.[15] The policy is to maintain a careful balance among the major immigration streams as follows: 50 percent social (family members); 25 percent humanitarian (refugees); and 25 percent economic (selected workers).[16]

Although family and refugee immigration are the traditional cornerstones of Canadian immigration, immigration for economic objectives is probably the most notable feature of the system. Such immigration includes selected workers and business investors or entrepreneurs,[17] and relies on a point system (see Table 2) to select them. Points are awarded to applicants for a set of skills and characteristics viewed to be good predictors of successful economic adaptation. These "units of assessment" cover nine areas that include education, age, occupation, experience, arranged employment, and language skills. The maximum number of points is 100; applicants must receive at least 70 for consideration.[18]

With regard to family immigration, Canada's definition of relatives is very inclusive and both Canadian citizens and permanent residents can apply for immigration on behalf of their relatives.[19] The critical prerequisite is sponsorship for incoming relatives. It entails an income requirement and agreement to be financially responsible for the beneficiary for up to ten years. This requirement helps pace the rate and volume of applications made by Canadians on behalf of their foreign relatives, minimize the public costs of newcomers, and insure that family unity objectives are upheld.

The humanitarian immigrant stream gives considerable flexibility to government officials to respond to international humanitarian situations. It provides for the admission not only of refugees who meet the United Nations Convention definition, but for two other groups, called Designated Class refugees and Humanitarian Entrants. These latter groups are people who are displaced or oppressed and in "refugee-like" situations but who do not meet the stricter Convention refugee definition.

Countries from which refugee-like persons have typically come include Guatemala, Lebanon and Sri Lanka. Applications for refugee resettlement among any of the refugee groups can be made from within or outside Canada.

Overall, the countries of origin for refugees in Canada are dramatically different than those from which refugees are resettled in the United States. This reflects differing foreign policy objectives, as they become translated into refugee programs, and different patterns of movement by asylum-seekers. Such striking differences between neighboring countries with so many similarities in their immigration traditions illustrate how selective and how rooted in history and policy migration patterns can be.

Other salient aspects of Canadian immigration and its impacts upon society are as follows:

- Present-day immigration is 42 percent Asian, 26 percent European, 17 percent from the Americas, and 15 percent from Africa and the Middle East; in 1961, 85 percent of Canada's immigration was from Europe and the United States.[20]

- A majority of today's immigrants settle in Ontario (about 54 percent), followed by Quebec (about 19 percent), British Columbia (14 percent), and Alberta (9 percent). Moreover, immigrants are

FIGURE 1
Canadian 1991 Immigrant Streams

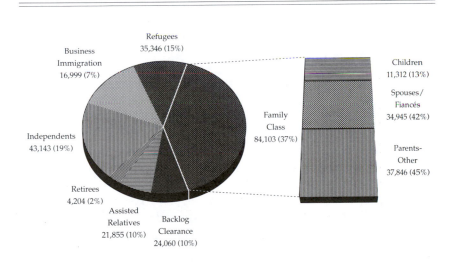

Source: Immigration Executive Reference File 1991 (preliminary data), prepared by Strategic Analysis, Strategic Planning & Research Directorate, Employment and Immigration Canada

heavily concentrated in cities with populations over 500,000, with almost 60 percent living in Toronto, Montreal, and Vancouver.[21] Officials have consistently tried to channel immigrants to less densely populated areas, with little success.

- The only distinction between Canadian citizens and permanent residents is the right to vote. Citizenship is achieved by birth (to native or foreign-born parents) or naturalization. Eligibility for naturalization requires one to be at least 18 years of age, with permanent residence for three years and knowledge of one of Canada's languages and of Canadian history, government and geography.[22]

- All permanent residents are entitled to the same benefits. About one-third of the refugees (termed "government-assisted") receive additional forms of assistance.

Altogether, Canada's immigration policy has been steadily honed and adjusted to embody a workable balance between generosity and economic self-interest. This balance is the linchpin for the policy's political support and credibility; Canada's geographical location strengthens its ability to manage flows in accordance with the nation's needs.

2. Issues of Special Interest

From a comparative standpoint, two elements of the Canadian experience are of particular interest for other Trilateral countries. They are the political asylum decision system and Canada's policy for integrating immigrants.

a. Political Asylum Decision System

As occurred in most industrialized countries during the 1980s, political asylum applications soared in Canada. Canada's refugee determination system, part of the Immigration Ministry, was not equipped to handle the increasing numbers. This resulted in severe delays which, in turn, encouraged applications from those not in genuine need of protection, further paralyzing the system. In 1988, Canada enacted sweeping legislation designed to establish a system that would deliver timely, fair refugee status determinations. Called the Immigration and Refugee Board (IRB), it is an independent tribunal, now the largest in Canada.

The Board administers a two-stage review process. The first stage takes place at the point of entry, where asylum applicants are given a preliminary hearing before an immigration border official and a

Board member to screen out claims that are "manifestly unfounded." Such a determination requires agreement by both officials. If one or both believes that the applicant's case deserves full consideration, s/he is admitted and referred for a full, in-depth assessment at a hearing.

The Board has about 250 members, who are located around the country but concentrated in the areas of high immigrant populations. They sit in panels of two to decide refugee claims. A positive decision by either one is sufficient to establish refugee status.[23] Applicants are represented by counsel provided at government expense. Board members have staff, who prepare the cases, and access to a documentation center, which is an information system on country conditions that is continuously updated by a professional research staff. By and large, cases are decided within six months, and processing of the backlog of 95,000 cases that had buckled the prior system was finally completed by the end of 1992.

Canada's effort to respond to the central migration development of the last decade—the political asylum crisis—has been both the most ambitious and the most successful in the world. Canada recognized that its entire immigration program was in jeopardy if the asylum caseload could not be effectively managed, because the public was beginning to doubt the government's ability to regulate immigration processes effectively.

Having created a new structure, the government appointed a chairman who was a well-known, respected, and very independent-minded Parliamentarian. The Chairman's effort to attract Board members broadly representative of Canadian society resulted in 26 percent of the Board's membership being comprised of "visible minorities;" only 10 percent were lawyers. This provided exceptional credibility for the system in the eyes of the refugee advocacy community, whose cooperation and support were essential to make the system work.

In 1989, its first year of operation, 88 percent of the cases were approved. This exceptionally generous approval rate reflected inexperience, but it also helped win public confidence. By late 1992, the percentage had gradually declined to 61 percent (see Figure 2). Moreover, the number of new applications has declined, presumably because frivolous claims have been discouraged. New legislation, approved in 1993, has eliminated the preliminary hearing. With over 95 percent of claimants found to be eligible for the full hearing, it proved to be ineffective and costly.

FIGURE 2
Canadian Acceptance Rate
(full hearing stage*)

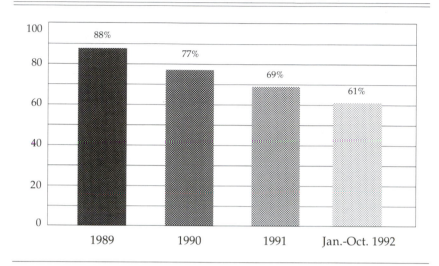

Source: Summary of Immigration and Refugee Board Activities, December 1992.
*including withdrawn and abandoned cases

The system is not without problems. Removals of those denied are not always successful, appeals take too long, and the system is very expensive.[24] Moreover, almost one-third of Canadian applicants enter Canada through the United States. For this reason, Canada is pressing to conclude a bilateral asylum agreement wherein the United States would agree to adjudicate cases of those who arrive there first. Applying such a "safe country" principle is patterned after developments in Europe. These parallel initiatives in Europe and North America could someday converge to create a multilateral asylum regime.

Overall, Canada has achieved what no other nation has been able to in the political asylum arena: it has a system that is timely and perceived to be fair. These are the twin characteristics that are required if nations are to both uphold international refugee standards and discourage unfounded claims.

b. Integrating Immigrants
Canada's rate of immigrant admissions poses formidable challenges for the society in integrating newcomers. A generous immigration

program cannot be sustained unless integration is successful. Canada's approach to the task is its policy of multiculturalism.

The aim is to promote mutual respect and a shared sense of identity among Canadians, dispel misconceptions about those who come, fight racism, and encourage the full participation of Canadians of all origins in the life of the society. The responsibility for these efforts resides with a specialized ministry that attempts to reach both Canadians-by-birth and newcomers.

Successful integration is a complex, continuing process, requiring adjustments by immigrants, established residents, and institutions alike. It asks that the immigrant learn and accept Canadian values at the same time that Canadians offer help and awareness of diverse cultures. The impulse is noble but its practice can be confounding, as these examples show:

- Somali culture teaches males not to obey females, making classroom discipline, with predominantly female teachers, a serious problem. Schools typically are places where the clashes in values arise and must be confronted.

- Similarly, health practices and norms represent flashpoints. Canadian physicians wrestle with, and try to prevent, female circumcision rites that can cause profound health and psychological damage to young women.

- Established populations feel threatened when immigrants move into particular areas and seem to take over. Yet, the separateness often is a survival mechanism that counteracts employment discrimination or unofficial housing discrimination.

In spite of serious difficulties like these, all available measures show the record of immigrant integration to be very good. The most important ingredient is language capability in English or French, Canada's official languages. Extensive language training opportunities are provided for immigrants at government expense, in close coordination with provincial governments and other institutions. Over the next decade, as many as 50 percent of new labor force entrants will be immigrants. It is strongly in Canada's interest, therefore, to insure that these people have the language capability required to cope in the workplace. Other available services include reception and orientation programs, translation, counselling and employment-related assistance.[25]

Nevertheless, multiculturalism is the most hotly debated aspect of the immigration question. Opposing schools of thought contend that public money is (a) reinforcing ethnic separateness and is, therefore, wrong, or (b) effectively helping groups integrate as a realistic response to a changing Canada. The concern in Canada, vividly exhibited in the failure of the October 1992 referendum to ratify an important Constitutional proposal, is that the nation has been so absorbed with being multicultural that shared values are being forgotten. These are inherent tensions to which immigration and integration give rise.

Canada devotes an exceptional degree of attention to the complexity of the integration challenge. This reflects a history of identifying the values of other cultures and the contributions of different peoples. The existing culture is thereby broadened to incorporate them, changes, and becomes stronger.

C. THE UNITED STATES

Always an ethnically mixed society, the United States is more so now than at any prior time. Net immigration, including illegal immigration, is about one million annually, with almost 90 percent from countries in Asia and the Americas.[26] Although U.S. law sets numerical ceilings or quotas for immigration, refugees, certain categories of family members, and some other groups are exempt. So, the numbers fluctuate somewhat from year to year.

Other key characteristics of U.S. immigration today are:

• Family reunification is the first priority of U.S. policy.[27] About 68 percent immigrate through family connections in the United States; about 15 percent are resettled as refugees; and about 17 percent are admitted because of skills they bring.

• Ten countries account for three-fourths of the immigrants. The leading source country is Mexico, followed by the Philippines, the FSU, Vietnam, Haiti, El Salvador, India, the Dominican Republic, China, and Korea.[28]

• More than three-fourths settle in California, Texas, New York, Florida, Illinois, and New Jersey, which are also among the largest states in the nation.

Until recently, the laws governing immigration were changed infrequently. The first restrictions did not come until 1875 when particular classes of immigrants (criminals and prostitutes) were declared ineligible. Numerical restrictions were not established until the isolationist fervor of the 1920s.

Two other major pieces of legislation were enacted in 1952, when the fear of Communism introduced ideological restrictions into immigrant admissions criteria, and in 1965, when the civil rights movement led to repeal of immigration quotas based on nationality as the basis for immigrant selection.

These national origin quotas were replaced by a system of quotas and preferences that favored family-based admissions, allowed for those with needed skills, authorized the same admissions level for all countries, and established an annual worldwide quota. These changes provided the basis for the substantial levels and new sources of immigration the United States is experiencing today.

The pattern of infrequent immigration legislation changed abruptly in the 1980s when three significant pieces of legislation were enacted:

- *The Refugee Act of 1980* provided for refugee admissions to be a permanent element of immigration by providing for government consultations to establish the annual level and countries of origin of refugees, and for programs and resources for resettling refugees.

- *The Immigration Reform and Control Act of 1986 (IRCA)* responded to growing illegal immigration by establishing penalties against employers who hire illegal immigrants and legalizing those illegally in the country before 1982 (or 1986, in the case of agricultural workers).

- *The Immigration Act of 1990* revised the quota preference system to provide substantially more immigration of skilled workers, more "slots" to reduce delays for certain groups of immigration-eligible family members, and greater diversity in the countries of origin of immigrants. These changes have increased immigration by about 35 percent annually and are the most comprehensive revision of immigration law since the 1965 act.

Taken together, these laws constitute a major revision that updated the nation's immigration policy and strongly endorsed an important continuing role for immigration in the 1990s. Further changes are likely to occur more frequently in the future, as the impacts of immigration on the society spark examinations that require adjustments in immigration laws.

There are many aspects of the U.S. immigration experience that are fascinating to examine in greater detail. The four that follow are of interest in a Trilateral context.

TABLE 3
**U.S. Annual Legal Immigration Levels
Under the Immigration Act of 1990**

	1992-1994 fiscal years	1995 and following
Family Stream	**465,000**	**543,000**
immediate relatives of U.S. citizens	264,000	317,000
family preferences	226,000	226,000
1st preference	*23,400*	*23,400*
2nd preference	*114,200*	*114,200*
4th preference	*23,400*	*23,400*
5th preference	*65,000*	*65,000*
Independent Stream	**140,000**	**140,000**
special immigrants	10,000	10,000
medical workers	—	—
employment-based workers	120,000	120,000
high-level professionals	*80,000*	*80,000*
entry-level professionals and skilled and unskilled workers	*40,000*	*40,000*
investors	10,000	10,000
point system immigrants	—	—
Diversity (begins in 1995)	—	**55,000**
Transitional Visas	**107,000**	—
adversely affected countries (1992-94)	40,000	—
displaced aliens (East Europe & Tibet)(1991-93)	—	—
Africa (1991-93)	—	—
preference backlog reductions	—	—
employees of U.S. businesses operating in Hong Kong (1992-94)	12,000	—
spouses and children of aliens legalized under IRCA (1992-94)	55,000	—
Miscellaneous	**2,000**	—
TOTAL (excluding refugees)	**714,000**	**738,000**

Source: The Immigration Act of 1990, P.L. 101-649

1. Illegal Immigration

Illegal immigration to the United States is by and large from Mexico. Hundreds of thousands of people without proper documents cross the 1800-mile border that divides the two countries each year. The illegal population also increasingly includes Central Americans and others who (generally with the help of smugglers) make their way through Mexico to the border, as well as people who have overstayed their visas.

The origins of Mexican illegal immigration lie in (a) the contiguity of two countries with among the highest income differentials of any neighboring countries in the world;[29] and (b) a history of labor recruitment in Mexico, especially for U.S. agriculture, that culminated in a guestworker program for farm workers, known as the Bracero program, from 1941 to 1964. It established strong binational economic linkages and labor market and family connections that have been resistant to subsequent policy changes.

Levels of illegal immigration steadily increased during the 1970s into the 1980s, with border apprehensions reaching an all-time high in 1986 of 1.6 million.[30] Although the economy was growing and most illegal immigrants readily found work, public concern steadily grew, culminating in the enactment of the 1986 legislation noted above. Its objective was to strengthen controls over illegal flows by making employers subject to fines and imprisonment for hiring illegal workers. Thus, the strategy of preventing entry through border control was augmented with the introduction of a new labor standard—legal status as a work eligibility requirement—in an effort to decrease the availability of jobs as an incentive for illegal immigration. The balancing measure for strengthened enforcement was a legalization program, through which three million people have regularized their status in the United States (see Table 4).

In addition to providing a needed enforcement tool, employer penalties represented a psychological watershed in the politics of immigration policy-making. As the chairman of a distinguished study panel that endorsed the legislation remarked, "We must close the back door in order to open the front door." Indeed, fundamental change in the system for legally admitting immigrants was needed. But politically, it could not be done until the government confronted the challenge of illegal flows. Above all, illegal immigration had begun contributing to national unease about an America newly vulnerable to events beyond its control. Enacting employer penalties helped restore confidence in the government's ability and

TABLE 4
Legalization Applicants under
The Immigration Reform and Control Act of 1986 (IRCA)
(by country of citizenship and type of application, December 1, 1991)

	Total	I-687*	I-700†
All Countries	**3,033,179**	**1,760,201**	**1,272,978**
North America**	**2,688,509**	**1,535,107**	**1,153,402**
Mexico	2,267,330	1,228,363	1,038,967
Caribbean	123,316	59,842	63,474
The Dominican Republic	*28,158*	*18,279*	*9,879*
Haiti	*59,846*	*15,942*	*43,904*
Jamaica	*19,151*	*12,961*	*6,190*
Other	*16,161*	*12,660*	*3,501*
Central America	**286,115**	**235,879**	**50,236**
Belize	6,250	6,119	131
Costa Rica	3,781	3,116	665
El Salvador	168,014	143,024	24,990
Guatemala	70,967	52,550	18,417
Honduras	18,121	13,056	5,065
Nicaragua	16,759	16,005	754
Other	2,223	2,009	214
South America	**103,674**	**73,850**	**29,824**
Argentina	5,991	5,112	879
Brazil	7,748	1,761	5,987
Colombia	34,748	26,363	8,385
Ecuador	16,302	13,211	3,091
Chile	4,880	4,148	732
Peru	19,743	12,674	7,069
Other	14,262	10,581	3,681
Asia	**148,317**	**80,380**	**67,937**
Bangladesh	7,604	1,328	6,276
China, Mainland	11,250	8,687	2,563
India	21,832	3,851	17,981
Iran	15,275	14,631	644
Korea	11,425	5,781	5,644
Pakistan	21,885	5,261	16,624
Philippines	29,385	19,071	10,314
Other	29,661	21,770	7,891
Europe	**40,566**	**35,332**	**5,234**

Source: U.S. Department of Justice, Immigration and Naturalization Service (INS), 1991

* applicants under the general legalization provisions of IRCA
† applicants under the special agricultural worker (SAWs) provisions of IRCA
** does not include figures for Canada and Greenland

commitment to control one element of its fate. As a result, although illegal immigration flows remain high, the continuing debate about illegal immigration is more realistic, informed, and susceptible to generosity in other areas of immigration policy.

Despite the political importance of enacting employer sanctions, their enforcement is not working well. The size of the illegal population in the United States is now close to that of the pre-1986 period. Wages have not increased in low-wage labor markets as they should if tighter labor standards were having an effect. There has been a resurgence of illegal sweatshops in industries like garment manufacturing that have traditionally employed predominantly immigrant workers. And there is some evidence that sanctions may heighten discrimination against non-white workers. These factors have led some labor unions and the nation's major civil rights organizations to call for repeal of the employer penalty law and repeal legislation is now under consideration by the U.S. Congress.

Although the government's enforcement of employer penalties has been weak, the central flaw in the sanctions scheme that was enacted is the absence of requirements for secure identity documents. If employers are to verify that their workers are legal, workers must have a document of some kind to prove to employers that their status is legal. Because a universal identification document does not exist in the United States, the law allows a wide range of documents to be used to meet the verification requirement. Most of the permissible documents can be readily counterfeited. Therefore, the use of fraudulent documents is widespread.

At the same time, new labor standards traditionally have taken a decade or more to become effective after being introduced. Proponents of employer penalties understood that the legislation was but a first step that would have to be strengthened over time. They also appreciated the special political sensitivity surrounding workable document requirements and were unable to produce all that they desired with the legislation in the face of it.

Thus, the ability of the United States to control illegal immigration turns to an important extent on the seemingly remote, esoteric issue of identity documents. This issue, in turn, raises warning flags in the American mind about government control versus individual freedom. Proposals to improve document security or introduce a universal identifier in the name of quelling illegal immigration are widely perceived as a cure that is worse than the disease.

The debate about illegal immigration is reviving because the United States has been unable to measurably limit illegal flows at a time of sluggish growth and broad-based economic restructuring. New solutions will require Americans to make decisions on trade-offs between the commitment to a generous but controlled immigration system and principles of individual freedom as they have been traditionally practiced and perceived.

2. Refugee Policy

Although based on deeply held humanitarian beliefs, U.S. refugee policy since World War II has also been a singleminded extension of Cold War antagonisms. Large numbers of refugees have been admitted from then-Communist countries and very few from elsewhere, even though severe, widespread human rights abuses have occurred in Haiti and El Salvador, for example, for which the United States is the likely country of asylum or resettlement. U.S. policy presented escapees from Communism as heroes because their flight underscored the repression which the West decried. At the same time, it treated most victims of right-wing dictatorships as illegal immigrants because compassion was seen as inconsistent with the political support such regimes enjoyed because they were anti-Communist.

With the Cold War behind, U.S. refugee policy has lost its rationale and refugee admissions are increasingly anachronistic. Although the annual level of admissions increased during fiscal years 1989 to 1992 from 107,000 to 132,000, more than 80 percent of the refugees being admitted are from the FSU and Vietnam.[31] And for both countries, the United States interviews refugees inside the country of origin. When in-country processing was introduced, it represented a pragmatic alternative to dangerous, chaotic escapes from oppressive regimes. Today, it serves largely to screen applicants that have an historical claim to U.S. compassion but are not in imminent danger or being singled out for abuse.

Against this backdrop, terrible humanitarian emergencies have arisen in ex-Yugoslavia, Somalia, northern Iraq and elsewhere. Neither the United States nor other nations have offered sizeable resettlement in response, preferring to address the humanitarian conditions in place. This is not inappropriate. However, it points to a critical question: What national interests and international norms should guide U.S. decisions about refugee relief and resettlement now that the Cold War has ended?

TABLE 5
U.S. Refugee Approval Rates
(by region and selected nationality, fiscal year '92*)

	Approval Rate for Cases Decided	Cases Approved	Cases Denied	Cases Pending
TOTAL	**89.1%**	**113,697**	**13,910**	**17,233**
U.S.S.R.	**96.6%**	**65,579**	**2,316**	**446**
East Asia/Pacific	**95.6%**	**31,751**	**1,467**	**101**
Laos	97.8%	6,210	138	1
Vietnam	95.2%	25,460	1,289	99
Cambodia	84.2%	48	9	1
Burma	50.0%	30	30	0
Africa	**77.8%**	**5,668**	**1,621**	**6,361**
Zaire	97.0%	97	3	434
Somalia	90.7%	1,583	162	1,519
Liberia	89.2%	637	77	793
Sudan	88.9%	120	15	312
South Africa	79.2%	19	5	13
Ehiopia	71.6%	3,116	1,237	2,887
Uganda	46.1%	88	103	351
Mozambique	7.7%	1	12	17
Latin America/Caribbean	**61.4%**	**2,493**	**1,566**	**2,344**
Cuba	89.7%	2,475	285	1,466
Haiti	1.2%	16	1,281	828
Eastern Europe	**54.9%**	**2,547**	**2,089**	**2,310**
Poland	100.0%	134	0	638
Czechoslovakia	100.0%	18	0	50
Albania	55.9%	1,104	870	864
Romania	52.5%	1,176	1,064	653
Bulgaria	42.5%	114	154	87
Near East/South Asia	**53.8%**	**5,659**	**4,851**	**5,671**
Iraq	60.5%	2,381	1,552	2,327
Iran	50.3%	1,823	1,799	1,109
Afghanistan	49.2%	1,455	1,500	2,234

Source: U.S. Department of Justice, Immigration and Naturalization Service (INS). Adapted from a tabulation by the U.S. Committee for Refugees.

Note: The overall total includes all nationalities. Nationalities for which fewer than than a total of ten cases were approved or denied are not included in the country-by-country listing.

* preliminary figures

Not only has the United States not answered the question, policy-makers seem quite comfortable with the status quo. One reason is that existing refugee admissions arrangements have the strong support of established domestic ethnic communities. They advocate effectively to perpetuate a program that has become largely an alternate immigration flow. This, combined with the absence of an international strategic outlook that is enhanced by refugee resettlement, has produced stagnation in a policy arena where the United States has typically provided aggressive, high-minded leadership.

Official complacency is not likely to persist in the face of spectacular incidents like the failed landing in June 1993 of the Golden Venture, a freighter that carried almost 300 Chinese aliens on a four-month sea journey so they could file political asylum applications upon arrival. In the end, eight perished as the group was forced to swim through frigid, choppy waters to the New York shore. But their incentive to try was based on the knowledge of their smugglers that asylum is granted to those who profess opposition to China's one-child population policy. Reconciling international human rights imperatives, changing foreign policies, and claims for refugee treatment in circumstances like these is a new reality that the government has not begun to grasp nor address. If it fails to do so, public anxiety could push Congress to enact measures that would have unfortunate consequences for the humanitarian traditions and leadership America has prized.

Among other things, what the United States needs is a humanitarian admissions approach, like that of Canada, through which to admit steadily decreasing numbers from groups that are changing from refugee to immigration flows. It needs to target refugee resettlement efforts to situations of acute need, such as Bosnian detention camp prisoners or targets of abuse by Haitian military officials, where its leadership signals opprobrium for egregious human rights abuse and the need for reform in the way that welcoming victims of Communism made a clear statement of principle during the years of the Cold War. And it needs to examine carefully questions surrounding the nature of political persecution in a changing world and how refugee policy can and cannot respond.

Because the United States is a destination for asylum-seekers, a major refugee resettlement nation, and a primary donor to humanitarian organizations, its behavior on refugee matters is important. It has traditionally helped set an international standard for other nations.

3. Immigrant Integration

The United States approaches matters of immigrant adaptation or integration very differently from Canada. With the exception of refugees, who are the beneficiaries of designated programs and services financed by the federal government,[32] U.S. integration policy has been to rely on a healthy economy and the vitality of public institutions, such as the education system, to provide opportunity and training that brings newcomers into the mainstream of American life. This non-policy, as it were, has worked surprisingly well.

Disturbing signs are appearing, however. One concerns English language training. Language ability is critical to economic success, the key barometer of immigrant integration. And economic success now depends increasingly on skills and training beyond high-school-level attainment. Yet one-half of Boston's schoolchildren, one-half of the population of Miami, and one million Los Angeles residents are English-deficient at a time when funding for bilingual education has been halved and actual federal spending for language instruction is only about $300 million.[33] Moreover, immigrants overwhelmingly want to learn the language, work hard to do so, and understand that their own success, and particularly the success of their children, depends upon fluency in English. The problem is not the immigrant; it is that instruction is not broadly available.

This is one of a set of key issues that must be more effectively addressed in the United States as it grapples with historically high immigration levels. Typically, the first generation is never truly integrated and finds protection in ethnic communities from the hardships of a new land. Where integration must work is with the second generation, that is, the children of immigrants. Immigrant children adopt the values and habits of the host culture. If they are successful in the terms those values and habits dictate, enjoy full membership, and have economic and social opportunities, integration is achieved. If they are spurned, they and their children are likely to reach back to rekindle an ethnic identity that gives them meaning. This can lead to serious alienation. The well-being of immigrant children, therefore, is of critical importance.

Immigrant enclaves in large cities are particularly interesting in this regard. Traditionally, ethnic communities in the United States have been a source of strength. Integration occurred as people moved from ethnic neighborhoods into the broader community over generations. However, the enclave becomes a ghetto when systems of labor and social mobility are closed, which is what has happened with large segments of the African-American population in the United States. The model of the enclave as a bridge to integration does not work in that case. Because today's immigration is dominated by different racial and ethnic groups, issues of mobility within the society are of paramount importance.

Immigrant integration is a two-way street. The immigrant changes to conform to society, as society changes to incorporate the immigrant. The well-known image of the melting pot to describe U.S. society has today been rejected in favor of that of a salad bowl or tapestry or mosaic. This is because the people of the United States have never melted together as one. It has been a country made up of groups with unique, differing characteristics and cultures that have been nurtured and celebrated as long as they did not violate broader democratic principles or responsibilities.

Thus, Sikhs can wear headcloths in prisons as an expression of religious belief, but Muslims may not practice polygamy. Amish people may use horses and buggies on local roads, but their children must attend school until the age of 16. Kosher and other religious rituals for preparing food can be practiced, but they must conform to public health standards and inspection requirements.

The tensions and dilemmas surrounding integration questions must continually be evaluated and negotiated. Today, they are manifesting themselves in debates about bilingual education in public schools, whether affirmative action obligations should encompass new immigrant groups, and reform of school curriculums to build greater tolerance for multiculturalism in society. The cultural debate that is inevitably sparked by immigration is probably the most difficult for societies to resolve. It is made far more manageable, however, when immigrants are making economic progress. This is where the U.S. experience has traditionally been successful and instructive.

Immigrant needs in education and other forms of investment in human capital coincide with those needed by the nation as a whole. If the society's public institutions can be revitalized and its racial tensions eased, the integration model that has worked well in the past should work well again. This requires a concerted commitment at all levels of society which must become a priority national effort for the 1990s.

4. Regional Economic Integration

Unlike the countries of the European Community, North America has just begun to walk the path of regional economic integration. And unlike the European Community, the aim of economic integration is economic growth, not a process for achieving political union.

With the exception of the temporary entry of business persons, migration issues are not an explicit element of the North American Free Trade Agreement (NAFTA), which incorporates the earlier U.S.-Canada Free Trade Agreement, nor is additional labor mobility presently envisioned for North America. Still, reducing migration pressures is regularly cited by all parties as one of the benefits of NAFTA. In President Salinas' words, "We want to send goods, not people."

In 1986, the U.S. Congress established a body known as the Commission for the Study of International Migration and Cooperative Economic Development. Its mandate was to look at policy responses to migration push forces. It concluded that job-creating growth in migrant-sending countries lessens the need people feel to emigrate. The most promising stimulus to future growth in sending countries is expanding trade between them and industrialized countries, particularly the United States. To the extent that NAFTA achieves the objective of expanded trade resulting in job creation, it will make a positive contribution to reversing migration pressures.

However, the Commission also noted that in the short-to-medium term, any measure to stimulate economic development is likely also to stimulate migration pressures. And "short-to-medium" in this connection is 10 to 20 years.[34] Some have called this phenomenon the "migration paradox." It results from the fact that development substitutes capital for labor, consolidates and often privatizes land, and introduces markets. These destroy traditional social and economic systems, displacing rural populations that become part of the large migrations that typically accompany development.[35]

Under NAFTA, this effect is to be cushioned significantly by provisions for a gradual adjustment of agriculture over a 15-year period. Tariffs will be phased out during a period in which large numbers of jobs should be created in other sectors of the economy. More generally and over the longer term, the effect of trade liberalization and development upon migration will be a function of the ways the economy and standards of living improve. Here the critical issue is wage differentials.[36]

Because per capita income is about ten times higher in the United States than in Mexico, Mexican wages must increase (narrowing wage differentials) and improved social well-being must be broadly experienced throughout Mexican society to discourage potential migrants from coming north. The U.S. International Trade

Commission's study on wage issues concluded that the wage gap would, indeed, diminish slightly, with the greater share of the adjustment occurring in Mexico.[37] If this happens, migration incentives should decline somewhat.

The threat to this outcome is if Mexico serves simply as a low-wage mecca for foreign investment. What is needed is targeted private investment and aggressive public investment in Mexican social programs and national infrastructure. With the strong migration networks and linked labor markets that presently exist between Mexico and the United States, the tradition and incentives that sustain migration must be met comprehensively with fundamental change.

The complexities of the development/migration nexus, particularly between nations that have strong migration links, mean that development cannot be seen simply as a substitute for migration or the avenue to eliminating it. Instead of arresting migration, development changes the character of migrations in important ways. The idea, therefore, that development prevents migrations must be modified to become an idea that accentuates the need to accept some level of migration as a relatively permanent, structural characteristic of cross-national economic interdependence. The realistic objective must be one of lessening the irregularity and unpredictability of illegal migration, not of averting migration completely.

The policy challenge is to combine development policy, international cooperation and migration dynamics in a coherent manner. The insight that should guide policy is that migration is closely bound up with the quality and type of development and cooperation that takes place. Trade liberalization will transform migration pressures only if it triggers sustainable rural development, upgrading of human capital, and broad civil rights protections for workers in North America's linked labor markets.

Seen this way, NAFTA is the first step in a continuing process, not an end in itself. An important next step would be to make immigration part of the NAFTA process by addressing labor standards. The effect of such measures would be to improve working conditions in Mexico, thereby improving the circumstances of workers who might otherwise come to the United States and diminishing the incentives of employers to locate in Mexico because of exploitive workplace conditions. This would be akin to the approach used by the European Community as it eliminated internal trade barriers.

In the end, NAFTA does not do anything to encourage immigration, either in the near or long term, beyond incentives that already exist.

And it does a great deal to create jobs and opportunities in the Mexican economy. At the same time, as economies become integrated and interdependent around the world, large differences in migration patterns ensue. Generally, migrations between and among them grow. Deepening economic differences among the nations of North America are not defensible and are not in our interest. But political leaders and publics must begin to acknowledge and grapple with the reality of migrations as a permanent feature of an economically interdependent world. The hope is that with measures such as NAFTA, those migrations become increasingly regulated and reciprocal, replacing their furtive, underground character of today.

*   *   *

Immigration nations have by no means solved the problems of immigration control, asylum case backlogs, or social tension between established and newcomer communities. They are inherently contentious issues. But the majority of the population has confidence in the government's ability to manage migration flows. This is because immigrant integration continues to be successful and because there are explicit laws, policies and administrative structures for regulating immigration processes, channelling public debate, and crafting political consensus.

III. European Community Countries

Centuries earlier than Canada and the United States, Western Europe too was populated by successive migrations from eastern locales. As a result, no Western European nation today is ethnically pure. Although differences among a wide array of distinct groups persist and often have important political impacts, they do not spark wars and are largely manageable within the parameters of the nation-state. Thus, many groups nurture strong cultural identities and ethnic pride, but also live and work peaceably with other groups and rely on democratic political structures to address their grievances.[38]

During the 19th and early 20th centuries, Europe experienced significant, sometimes massive, emigration to the New World. From 1850 to 1920, more than 50 million people, about 12 percent of Europe's total population, left. However, for some countries the outflow was much higher. Forty percent of the population of the British Isles left; and 30 percent left Italy and the Scandinavian countries. Emigration of surplus populations played an essential role in Europe's industrial revolution, contributing to its transformation from an agricultural society to a modern economy. As such, migrations were intrinsic to development and modernization processes, just as they are for many developing countries today.

The post-World War II period established the context for today's migration panorama in Western Europe. Guestworker policies to rebuild war-ravaged, labor-short economies combined with special residency privileges for inhabitants of some former colonies brought substantial numbers of non-Europeans to the continent. A significant proportion have become citizens or long-time residents, bringing family members and different traditions to their adoptive homelands.

Most recently, migrations from Eastern Europe pierced the Iron Curtain, proclaiming the end of the Cold War. Indeed, the process of mass population movements played an important role in the dismantling of the Berlin Wall, the Cold War's most powerful symbol.

Today, Europe stands at the very crossroads of international migration pressures. It faces urgent demands from across the Oder-Neisse River to the east and the Mediterranean Sea to the south.

A. EUROPE AND IMMIGRATION TODAY

1. The Foreigner Issue

Although not perceiving itself as a region of immigration, European nations have steadily become home to substantial and growing numbers of foreigners.

a. The Profile

Numbering almost 16 million, the foreigner population represented well over 4 percent of the population of the European Community (EC) at the beginning of 1991. As Table 6 indicates, the largest share of non-nationals—about one-third—were citizens of other European Community states (citizens of an EC country have a right to residence and work permits in another member country). Turkish citizens constituted another 14 percent of non-nationals—Turkey is the largest single immigrant-supplying country. Citizens of Morocco, Algeria and Tunisia represented over 12 percent of the total.

The trend is toward an increasing proportion from non-EC, less developed countries.[39] This is because internal EC migration is not expected to increase appreciably, despite differences in material living standards among some EC countries, and because pressures to migrate from outside Western Europe are increasingly strong. In addition, Europe is host to a dramatic increase in numbers of asylum applicants, and a growing population of illegal immigrants that now numbers about 2.7 million, according to International Labor Organization (ILO) estimates.[40] Some countries, such as Italy, host greater numbers of illegal than legal non-EC residents.[41]

These are historically new phenomena for Europeans. They have generated an immigration debate that is as much a reaction to changes immigration has already created as it is to the prospect of additional newcomers. Those who have arrived and those continuing to come are seen by many citizens as emissaries of distant cultures with significantly different social values that are incompatible with European societies. This response creates a paradox, for Europe's self-image is that of having established liberal, open societies.

Foreigners from outside the EC are concentrated in France and Germany, the two countries that most actively recruited guestworkers through programs that were considered temporary labor market measures. These two, with somewhat over one-third of the EC population, have two-thirds of the non-EC foreigner population. For both, Islamic immigrants are about one-third of their foreign

TABLE 6
Foreign Residents in EC Countries
(by citizenship, in thousands, on 1 January 1991)

Total Non-Nationals	**15,906**	*100%*
EC Nationals	**5,756**	*36%*
Non-EC Nationals	**10,150**	*64%*
Turkey	2,247.8	*14.1%*
Morocco	1,053.4	*6.6%*
Algeria	640.8	*4.0%*
Tunisia	283.7	*1.8%*
Yugoslavia	785.3	*4.9%*
Poland	368.4	*2.3%*
Romania	78.5	
ex-USSR	52.5	
India	195.2	*1.2%*
Iran	170.0	*1.1%*
Pakistan	140.8	
Vietnam	98.5	
Philippines	94.8	
Sri Lanka	94.5	
Lebanon	87.8	
United States	357.0	*2.2%*
Japan	81.6	
Canada	59.9	
Austria	212.4	*1.3%*
Switzerland	98.7	
Sweden	60.2	
Stateless and Unknown	911.7	*5.7%*

Source: Adapted from Eurostat, "Population and Social Conditions," *Rapid Reports* 1993:6, Table 1. Undocumented residents are not included.

populations and are seen to pose major dilemmas where immigrant integration issues are concerned.

France, with a foreign-born population of 7.3 percent, has the largest proportion of foreign-born in the EC, a trend that has remained fairly constant since the early 1970s. Thirty-eight percent are from EC countries, a portion that has decreased during the last decade as the percentage from Maghreb countries, Sub-Saharan Africa, Turkey and Asia is increasing. Foreign residents in Germany represent 7.2 percent of its population. This percentage includes non-German nationality residents and their German-born children, who retain the parents' nationality and are counted as foreigners. It does not include ethnic German newcomers from Eastern Europe and the FSU, who can claim German citizenship by law.[42] These figures place the two countries high in the ranks of immigrant countries globally and have occasioned the observation that foreigners now constitute the EC's 13th member state.

b. Historical Backdrop

Today's immigration patterns are the result of a combination of post-war policies and recent global trends. During the 1950s and 1960s, rebuilding and economic expansion led migrants to come from lagging countries to boom areas. Typically, workers came from southern Europe, Yugoslavia, Turkey, and the Maghreb countries of northern Africa, in response to organized labor recruitment policies, known as guestworker programs.

In 1973-74, as the postwar expansion slowed, guestworker recruitment from non-EC countries came to a halt. Officials no longer praised the benefits of a flexible alien workforce. Rising unemployment, in the wake of worldwide oil-price hikes, sent almost three million migrants home. However, many had settled in Western Europe with their families, and the propensity to stay was intensified by the end of formal recruitment.

Since the end of the guestworker programs, governments have declared that Europe is "closed" to immigration from outside of Europe. However, a steady, growing number of newcomers have entered European countries through authorized family unification programs for former guestworkers and other foreign residents, contract labor arrangements, illegal immigration, and political asylum application processes. The numbers that reside in Europe today as legacies of guestworker programs are higher than the number there when migrant workers were actively being recruited. This illustrates the power of immigrant networks as a dynamic of transnational processes. It further illustrates the substantial gap that has opened between political rhetoric and popular experience.

Moreover, whereas northern European countries had received labor from poorer southern European neighbors, all EC members (except Ireland) have now become immigrant-receiving states. Italy, Spain, and Portugal all have been the beneficiaries of changes that have transformed them from emigration to immigration nations in the very short span of 20-30 years. Unwittingly but unmistakably, Europe has become an immigration region.

2. East-West Pressures

Europe's newest migration pressures originate to the east, where the Cold War almost completely froze population movements for decades. Its end with the Eastern European revolutions in 1989 saw 1.2 million people leave the Warsaw Pact states in search of new lives in the West. In 1990, a dread that "the Russians are coming" swept across Europe, but the predicted chaos of emergency movements did not materialize. In 1991, the numbers from Eastern Europe showed signs of subsiding, as about 800,000 left. They included the "privileged ethnics," such as Germans, Jews, Greeks and Armenians, who emigrate through official channels; asylum-seekers; and 100,000-200,000 illegal immigrants.[43] In addition, the law that removed emigration restrictions in the FSU took effect in July 1991. While millions have now begun to travel for tourist or professional visits, the level of permanent emigration has somewhat abated.

However, with the war in ex-Yugoslavia, a massive population displacement of more than two million people has taken place within its republics. In addition, almost 600,000 have fled to Hungary, to the Czech Republic and Slovakia, and to other European countries—especially Germany, which hosts 250,000 of the war's victims. The Croatians and Bosnians, in particular, are anxious to return but cannot because their villages have been destroyed and occupied.

The principal factors underlying these flows include the following:

- *Pent-up demand.* The psychological impulse to move was overwhelming as a reaction to years of denied access to the West and a consistent message that whoever could cross a border would be welcomed. This was intensified by the idea that crossing a border was final, a permanent act which could not be retraced.

- *The search for hard-currency wages.* The largest group in this category of labor migrants was Poles who came especially to Germany, where temporary work was abundant and illegal employment was tolerated by the authorities. Romanians were the second largest group. Similarly, Russians and other citizens of former Soviet states, who were not subject to entry requirements by bloc countries, came to Poland in large numbers by 1991 to work and trade.

- *Stranded socialist cadres.* Residents of third world nations, such as Vietnam and Somalia, who had lived in bloc countries as visitors, contract laborers, students, military trainees, etc. suddenly faced dramatic new circumstances. Many returned, but many also wished to live in a united Germany or came to Western Europe, filing for political asylum to remain.

- *Ethnic tension and strife.* Historic grievances, new incidents, and armed outbreaks have sparked the migration of particular ethnic groups to places within the former Soviet space and to other Western states, particularly ethnic Germans to Germany. The greatest potential for emergency migrations in the future is within this realm, originating most likely in areas on the periphery of the FSU.[44]

East-West migration pressures will be longstanding as a function of both economic and humanitarian factors. The economic picture is one of difficult restructuring and requirements for heavy outside investment for many years to come. This will substantially increase unemployment. The contrast in standards of living with Western neighbors is stark. GDP per capita figures for Bulgaria, former Czechoslovakia, Hungary, Poland and Romania are only 13 percent of the EC average.[45] Some authoritative recent estimates posit 10 million would-be immigrants (four from Eastern Europe, six from the FSU) in the coming decade.[46]

As sobering as the economic projections are, it is humanitarian emergencies that represent the most dangerous migration scenario. The region suffers latent problems of displaced minorities, and militant nationalisms are on the rise. Ethnic wars are underway not only in ex-Yugoslavia but in several areas of the Caucasus and in Central Asia. Tensions are building against Hungarians in Slovakia, Romania, and Serbia and against Albanians in Kosovo and Macedonia. Other groups are similarly threatened, including many among the 25 million Russians living in other republics of the FSU. Those living in the Baltic states are particularly uneasy in the face of legislation that narrows citizenship eligibility and certain other of their rights. Some specific populations, like returning military, are getting special attention because of the potential instability their relocation could create. Germany has been especially helpful in providing aid to Russia for this relocation.

The dilemma is not limited to the possibility that refugees could overwhelm Western Europe. Sudden, sizeable emergency migrations within the East can undermine the authority and legitimacy of fragile elected governments and legislatures in newly democratizing states, particularly the Visegrad group of Poland, Hungary and the Czech and Slovak Republics. This possibility is fundamentally inimical to Western interests and explains why the defense of minority groups is becoming a central concern of Europe's multilateral institutions, such as the Council of Europe, the Conference for Security and Cooperation in Europe (CSCE), and the EC. These bodies have all begun to integrate into their decision-making the indissoluble link among borders, minorities and migrations.

If ethnic conflict can be ameliorated, East-West movements should eventually be able to be regulated within acceptable bounds. This has begun in some cases. By making its currency convertible and aggressively pursuing privatization, Poland has been able to quell the hemorrhage of its citizens. It has associated itself with the Schengen countries (see pages 56-57), acquiring a border without visas in exchange for agreeing to accept anyone rejected for admission into Germany and to receive all Polish citizens back without deportation procedures. One of the largest groups in the European asylum queue five years ago, Polish application numbers have fallen dramatically.

This example carries within it the seeds of the direction European policy can be expected to take. In addressing East-West migration pressures, EC countries are likely to pursue economic integration, steadily incorporating Eastern Europe into EC structures with their promise of political stability and economic improvement in the years ahead.

3. South-North Pressures

More longstanding and more deep-seated than migration pressures from the East are those from the South. For Europe, South-North migration pressures come primarily from nations on the Mediterranean rim, although there are also sizeable flows from more distant countries, such as Iran, Sri Lanka, and the Philippines.

Africa presents the most dire picture. Its population, now the fastest-growing in the world, will increase from 642 million in 1990 to almost 1.6 billion in 2025. At the same time, fertility rates in northern Africa are declining toward those of Europe, and peak birth rates for sub-Saharan Africa will occur at the turn of the century, decreasing thereafter.

A by-product of colonialism, international migration is a well-established tradition in many African countries, especially for educational purposes. Although some who went to Europe and elsewhere traditionally did not return, the trend today is for increasingly significant numbers of the more educated to leave. From 1960 to 1975, higher-educated Africans migrated at rates of about 1,800 a year. By 1987, the number reached 23,000. The benefits of human resource investments in education being made by poorer countries are being realized by developed countries, where growing numbers of those with education lead the productive years of their lives.

The Maghreb countries are the principal source of Africans coming to Europe. The motivation is primarily economic. Some come legally through family unification openings. More arrive and become part of the clandestine population. Of the 223,000 illegal migrants who registered for Italy's amnesty program in 1990, the majority were from northern Africa and Asia. A high proportion of Europe's illegal immigrant population is estimated to be from Africa. In the long run, the size of the illegal population in Europe is likely to increase faster than that of other categories of migrants. A growing number are from sub-Saharan Africa and use Maghreb countries as a pathway toward Europe.

More problematic than the numbers, perhaps, are the characteristics of the migrants themselves. Because Mediterranean rim countries are racially and religiously different from Europe, South-North migration accentuates the visibility of immigration and its implications for European societies. Serious social problems are arising as a result, and violence against migrants has disproportionately targeted those from less developed nations.

The crisis in the less developed world is deepening and must command greater attention. Europe has no real choice but to commit itself to assistance efforts that narrow the widening prosperity gap with Mediterranean rim societies. This is likely to take the form of closer economic association, however, instead of the more comprehensive strategy of economic integration that is unfolding where East-West presssures are concerned. Both Turkey and Morocco have requested Community membership, although Morocco has now postponed its request. Such applications are viewed as far down the line in comparison with the bids that will one day be made by countries like Hungary, Poland and the Czech Republic.

Nonetheless, an aggressive commitment to attacking the causes for South-North migration would require a reactivated Mediterranean policy, considerably more comprehensive than the existing Lomé Convention, which applies to African, Caribbean and Pacific states well beyond northern Africa. Formal association with Maghreb nations would lead to lower EC trade barriers, greater access to loans for balance of payments support, and similar measures. Special economic areas, akin to the kind of development that has taken place along the China coastline, should be established, as has already been successfully done in Tunisia.

An EC-Maghreb Association Agreement would most likely begin with Morocco. France and Spain should take leadership within the Community for efforts to establish Association agreements with other north African nations. Spain has concluded a readmission agreement with Morocco which is operating satisfactorily. Morocco has also taken measures to prevent illegal immigration into the Community.[47] Turkey is another obvious target country, with which Germany would play the lead role.

There are three major migration divides in the world: the Rio Grande, separating the United States and Latin America; the Oder-Neisse, separating Western and Eastern Europe; and the Mediterranean, separating Europe from Africa and the Middle East. The Mediterranean divide may not be a long-term one. With aggressive development efforts, the Maghreb, Egypt and Turkey could develop relatively quickly. The divide then would become the Sahara. This line between northern and sub-Saharan Africa is the real development rift to Europe's south.

The overall economic strategies Europe and the United States are pursuing, albeit for broader reasons, are likely to result in the creation across all three of these divides of more prosperous zones which will to some extent absorb migration pressures from more distant areas. Thus, Mexico would become such a zone for the rest of North America; and Poland, the Czech Republic, Hungary, the Maghreb and Turkey for Western Europe.

In this way, areas of extreme poverty would recede geographically from advanced industrial nations. This is not unlike what has happened in Western Europe during the past 25 years. European economic integration succeeded in raising standards of living in

Portugal, Spain, southern Italy, and Greece so that migration pressures no longer emanate from neighboring countries within Western Europe but from more distant locales. This increases the possibility of achieving, over time, more effective regulation of migration flows.

4. The Asylum Crisis

Of all the issues and new questions international migrations are posing for European nations, none is more urgent or explosive than the asylum crisis. The numbers of asylum applicants have increased by alarming proportions in European countries. In 1980, Europe's annual caseload was under 20,000. By 1992, it had reached 560,000 (see Table 7), more than a doubling since 1988 alone. The cost of processing applications and other services granted to asylum-seekers has been estimated to have been $6 billion in 1991, at least five times the UNHCR budget to care for more than 17 million refugees around the world.[48]

The early waves of asylum-seekers from Eastern Europe that appeared as the Iron Curtain fell have subsided, and it is now safe to return most East Europeans to their homelands because these countries are considered to have become democracies that no longer

TABLE 7
Asylum Applications in EC Countries, 1992

Germany	438,200	*78%*
France	26,800	*5%*
United Kingdom	24,600	*4%*
Belgium	17,650	*3%*
Netherlands	17,450	*3%*
Denmark	13,900	*2%*
Spain	12,650	*2%*
Luxembourg*	3,429	
Italy	2,500	
Greece	1,950	
Portugal	700	
Ireland	n/a	
TOTAL	**559,829**	*100%*

Source: UNHCR Regional Office for the European Institutions, Brussels, May 1993

*provisional figure

practice political persecution. The more problematic asylum population is composed of applicants from less developed countries. Five years ago, about 40 percent of asylum applications were approved. That proportion fell to 25 percent in 1991. Although there is considerable variation among states—approval rates in some are as low as two or three percent—three-quarters of the overall asylum-seeker population is found not to need protection, even after often-lengthy appeal procedures have been fully exhausted. Nonetheless, 80 percent of those who are rejected stay. The delays and inability to remove people who are found not to be eligible for refugee status are as damaging as the spiraling numbers of applications. They become, in themselves, an additional migration incentive.

The most objectionable policy in the public mind is one where the nation appears unable to control a basic element of sovereignty, such as the choice of who resides in the country. This abdication of choice is what burgeoning asylum caseloads represent, and long-staying asylum populations symbolize national vulnerability.

Asylum regimes that cannot deliver fair, timely decisions and that cannot remove those who are ineligible are de facto immigration schemes whereby individuals select the country, instead of the country selecting those who will join the society. When this occurs, as it has in Europe, protection for legitimate refugees is seriously jeopardized because the public believes its generosity is being exploited. Those who would abuse asylum procedures are encouraged to do so because they are not penalized. And the public loses confidence in the ability of government to carry out its core functions. This has consequences that reach far beyond the migration matters immediately at hand.

These dynamics are all at work in Germany which, with more than two-thirds of Europe's asylum-seekers, has borne the brunt of the crisis. To a lesser extent, its experience is typical for most parts of Western Europe. Germany's asylum population includes Romanian Gypsies (Roma and Sinti people), Turks, Bulgarians, Iranians, Nigerians, Vietnamese, Afghans, and Sri Lankans. In 1991, more than 438,000 applications were pending; the 1992 total rose to 590,000. In the first four months of 1993, new applications were filed at a rate of more than 1,400 per day.[49]

The asylum population is but one aspect of a larger immigration phenomenon. Since 1988, Germany has received slightly more than 1.5 million ethnic Germans from Poland, Romania, and the FSU.[50] To this must be added the numbers of Germans who have moved westward as part of unification processes.[51] These high rates are likely to be transitory. Nevertheless, the asylum crisis is the lightning rod for public dissatisfaction over these historic changes and has become one of the most prominent issues on the German domestic agenda.

Among the controversies and outbreaks it has sparked are the following:

- Acts of violence committed by rightist groups against foreigners numbered 2,285 in 1992, according to the federal police, a sharp increase over the previous year. The first four months of 1993 saw 670 attacks compared with 420 for that period of 1992. Seventeen deaths occurred in 1992; by May 1993, nine had been killed. The perpetrators have been angry young people who are without political ideology, except for a minority of neo-Nazis.[52]

- The most ominous incidents involved the planned fire-bombing of a hostel for asylum-seekers in Rostock, and the home of long-time Turkish-nationality residents in Mölln, killing two teenaged girls born in Germany and a grandmother. Most recently, five members of a Turkish household were burned to death in Solingen. The family had lived in the country for 23 years.[53]

- Police and public officials have been strenuously criticized for their failure to protect foreigners adequately.[54] German business leaders issued warnings that a rise of racism is hurting foreign investment and tourism. Millions took to the streets to express revulsion against the attacks. Chains of lights for tolerance became the symbol of opprobrium against prejudice and anti-Semitism in cities from Munich to Hamburg.

- Since the Mölln incident, the government has moved to ban neo-Nazi groups, a legal act under Germany's Constitution. Ten such organizations have been designated, of which two have now been outlawed.[55] Authorities took a series of other actions to stiffen the government's response. In one month, the numbers of attacks fell from 250 to 75.[56] Nevertheless, the more recent statistics have led to calls for an all-out counterattack like that mounted against leftist terrorists in the 1970s.

- The Solingen tragedy mobilized the long-quiet Turkish community, which numbers 1.8 million and is Germany's largest minority. Their leaders see Solingen as a turning point in the effort to win acceptance, calling for rights instead of official sympathy.[57]

Just days before Solingen, the German Bundestag enacted sweeping changes to its asylum policy by adopting an inter-party agreement to change the Constitution. On the day of the vote, the parliament building was surrounded by barricades of opponents to the change. To vote, many members got in only with the help of helicopters and boats. The scene effectively captured the fractiousness of the debate that the asylum crisis has unleashed in Germany.

"People persecuted on political grounds shall enjoy the right of asylum," read the 1949 Constitution, called the Basic Law. This protection was intended to prevent the recurrence of Nazi abuses. The provision was interpreted to mean that no limitations could be placed upon the right of asylum. Any foreigner arriving and claiming asylum was presumed to have a legitimate claim (and provided with housing and necessities) until an investigation proved otherwise. Once a point of national pride, the provision needed to be changed according to 70 percent surveyed in opinion polls.[58]

To the Social Democrats, whose agreement the ruling Christian Democrats needed for the required two-thirds majority, changing the Constitution represented a shameful concession to neo-Nazi brutality. However, after protracted debate and a long stalemate, the Social Democrats finally endorsed the position of their then leader, Bjorn Engholm, who had staked his claim to challenge Chancellor Kohl in 1994 on the vote. It cleared the way for discussions of an inter-party agreement upon which to base limited Constitutional change.

The new law, effective July 1, 1993, limits the legal avenues available to asylum-seekers and rejects admission at the borders to people from countries determined to be safe. It also cuts allowances to support applicants by 25 percent. Upon enactment, one party leader observed, "This decision is crucial for internal peace in our country."[59]

The nation with the biggest asylum burden has now also taken the most sweeping, agonizing steps of any European nation to respond. Even so, changing laws and procedures for handling asylum cases, either in Germany or elsewhere in Europe, will not be enough. And politicians would be wise not to promise an end to the asylum problem. That is because asylum systems are bearing the burden not just of refugees and refugee-like entrants, but of migration pressures overall.

Asylum serves as a significant legal channel into Europe for those with either humanitarian or economic reasons to leave their countries. With few other means of legitimate access and weak removal mechanisms, the asylum system not only screens refugees but also functions as an immigration system. Unfortunately, it is an ersatz immigration system, in that it allows a nation's newcomers to self-select.

B. IMMIGRATION AS AN ISSUE OF HIGH POLITICS

The European Community was on the brink of implementing its commitment to establish open internal borders as the need to respond more effectively to unanticipated migration pressures arose. The convergence of the two issues, along with the growing public backlash against uninvited immigrants, has made migration a matter of high politics in Europe. Europe sees immigration as inextricably bound up with its political, economic, and social well-being, as well as its future security interests. This is very different from the way immigration is perceived and debated in Canada and the United States, at least at the present time.

1. Parties and Domestic Politics

For several years, anti-foreigner political parties have been building a constituency on the political right around the issues of closing borders and expelling non-Europeans. France's National Front, led by Jean-Marie Le Pen, has achieved the most notoriety and the best electoral showings in this regard, but similar movements exist in Austria (Jörg Haider's Austrian Freedom Party), Germany (the Republicans) and elsewhere.

Single-mindedly xenophobic, these parties have defined the foreigner issue for the public, while the center parties have failed to provide a coherent, alternative voice in the debate. The inability of the mainline parties to explain the changes migrations are creating and propose practical responses has made governments appear helpless and ineffective. This has eroded the authority of political leaders, contributing to the gains anti-foreigner right-wing parties have made.

The shortcomings in official responses have been particularly evident where violence against foreigners is concerned. The German case provides the clearest illustration. Many of the right-wing youth who have provoked violence in Germany have suffered from the social upheaval of reunification. The economy, the family, education, the legal system—all are in crisis for them. Ultranationalism is arising throughout former bloc states where, though the foreign power is gone, foreigners are vilified and held responsible for society's problems.

However, this is an insufficient explanation. Although the most highly publicized incidents, such as Rostock, have taken place in eastern Germany, a greater number have occurred in western Germany. Characterizing these incidents as a problem of asylum overload against which disaffected youth are bound to rebel avoids confronting the basic problem, which is racism and xenophobia. Its resurgence jeopardizes the reputation for democracy that Germany has struggled for more than four decades to build.

The moment of deadly clarity in this regard came with the Mölln killings, where the victims were neither asylum-seekers nor outsiders. Finally, a public figure rose to the occasion when President Richard von Weizsäcker gave his Christmas message. He spoke of the crucial role foreigners play in the German economy.[60] He praised the hundreds of thousands who have taken to streets with candles to demonstrate against extremist violence. He called upon Germans to broaden their definition of citizenship and accept the country's six million Turkish and other foreign residents as Germans. And he illustrated how even the language excludes foreigners from the mainstream.

"Ten-year-old Yeliz Arslan was born among us, and never lived anywhere else. Our media simply called them three Turks. That expression, based solely on their passports, already suggests that they should remain forever foreign. But those three in Mölln belonged to us."[61]

It was one of the first direct pleas made by a prominent leader to explain events and to suggest the appropriate moral climate within which to assess them. In contrast, the prevailing political discourse has fed public fear and confusion by criticizing the "sounds" and "smells" of immigrants, defending homogeneity on the grounds that Europeans are "not used to black people coming in," or using slogans like "the boat is full."[62]

Unfortunately, the aftermath of the Solingen deaths has seen the government again define the new crisis as a police, not a political matter. Responding to calls for citizenship and broader rights for German-Turks, the Interior Minister said, "I am opposed to any mixing of different issues."[63]

Germany's experience has been the most painful, but it is symptomatic of Europe overall. The core difficulty is that Europe has become an immigration region, having neither planned nor chosen to be one. Leaders have been slow to grasp this new situation and its implications and have been unable or unwilling to take up questions regarding ways to regulate migration flows and manage cultural diversity. Even states that have accommodated substantial immigration, like France and Britain, steadfastly insist they are not immigration nations. Consequently, the policy debate that is needed about how immigration is changing European countries and the challenges that lie ahead has been occurring in the streets.

Instead of responding to the asylum crisis as a signal for broad new imperatives, political leaders have used it as a scapegoat for other national ailments, avoiding speaking openly about how Europe is changing. In the absence of a politics of reality, national conversations have not confronted issues like the importance of immigrants in Europe's economic well-being (despite high unemployment), the case for responding to refugees uprooted by conflicts along ethnic lines, the social value of immigrant family unification, or the true limitations democratic governments face in attempting to stop unwanted migrations.

Unless European politics are able to bring the full complexity of migration questions into the open and propose and critique comprehensive solutions, the gap between politics and public experience will continue to widen. Closing that gap is a threshold requirement for political leaders to embrace. Although nations individually have not performed admirably, Europe's collective efforts, through European Community and other collaborative activities, have begun to mobilize the kinds of responses and consensus that are needed to meet the challenge.

2. European Community Structures and Policy

Although immigration prerogatives are a classic expression of national sovereignty, European Community states are steadily ceding their national powers in this arena to European regional structures and cooperative mechanisms. This trend reflects a growing conviction at national levels that solutions to migration pressures must be found through international cooperation. It is a marked departure from just two or three years ago, when the habit was to rely on unilateral action, largely limited to entry controls. The sense of crisis that has permeated the issues has generated a dizzying array of gatherings and new initiatives. Altogether 100 official meetings and eight ministerial conferences took place in 1991, and the pace of such activity continues today.

The need for harmonization of Europe's policies toward migration springs from the process of European integration itself.

a. The Single European Act

The Treaty of Rome, which established the EC in 1957, guaranteed nationals of the six original member states the right to seek employment in other member states. This right became fully effective in 1968. A decade of slow growth and high unemployment led to the first major amendment to the Treaty, the Single European Act, which became effective in 1987. The objective of the Single Act was to promote economic growth by eliminating internal barriers among the now-twelve Community members by the end of 1992. Achieving the single market was to carry with it full implementation of the four freedoms outlined in the Rome Treaty—free movement of capital, goods, services and persons.

International migration raises issues that must be manageable for the entire Community. Shifting movements and their problems from one country to the other is neither judicious nor politically desirable. The difficulty is that non-EC nationals (see Table 6) are excluded from the freedom of settlement provisions. With the steep growth in their numbers and the political sensitivity surrounding foreigner issues, the policies and procedures guiding their access to the Community and the rights in other member states of those already residing in a member state have been hotly contested.

Thus, while most of the provisions of EC-1992 have proceeded on schedule, the freedom of movement provisions for persons were not implemented by December 31, 1992. This is because internal borders cannot be lifted until joint external border controls are in place. And putting joint external border controls into place has involved questions of cooperation among member states with a link to immigration issues which have not yet been satisfactorily resolved. Current estimates are that land and sea border checks, as well as airport checks, will be eliminated by the end of 1993.

Against the backdrop of EC-1992, a series of specific initiatives have been launched that, taken together, constitute the elements of a common migration policy. The coordinated efforts of Community nations began with technical measures intended to achieve common procedures. The Maastricht Treaty and its aftermath introduced for the first time a conceptual framework within which harmonization of substantive policy has begun. The critical instruments are as follows:[64]

The Schengen Convention was the first intergovernmental agreement in Europe to abolish internal borders. It introduced the idea (in 1985) of abolishing internal borders in favor of jointly agreed external border checks and procedures. It envisioned common visa requirements for entry from many non-Community countries and sophisticated information-exchange among signatories to allow for the exclusion of ineligible or undesirable persons from Schengen territory. This has consequences for regulating migratory flows.

Originally consisting of five EC member countries,[65] the Schengen Group's concept, especially as far as external border control is concerned, has been adopted by the EC as the method to be used for European border control under EC-1992. With Poland recently being associated with Schengen, the concept has now been extended beyond the EC. In addition, EC states have signed an agreement with most European Free Trade Association (EFTA) countries[66] that includes them in freedom of movement measures. Thus, nationals of what is known as the European Economic Area (EEA) are to be able to move freely throughout 18 European nations.

Although there are complex administrative preparations—including a centralized information system on undesirable individuals—required for full implementation of the Schengen agreement, the main obstacle to its progress has been political. Certain countries, especially Denmark and Great Britain, have been unwilling to eliminate immigration controls at their national borders for non-EC nationals. Although the matter remains unsettled, it seems that for the moment the Community will tolerate a two-track process[67] for Great Britain: one system of entry for EC nationals, and a separate system for non-EC citizens.

France's newly elected government has postponed its implementation of the Convention because it considers Italy and Greece to be countries which have not perfected their external border controls sufficiently. German ratification, delayed on constitutional grounds, has only just occurred (June 1993). And the de-criminalization of "soft drugs" in some Schengen countries has fed fears of dramatic increases in drug trafficking, which already accounts for more than half of all arrests in Europe.

The Dublin Convention, adopted in June 1990, addresses political asylum processing issues. It establishes the proposition that the country into which an asylum-seeker enters is responsible for processing the asylum claim[68] and that other member countries will accept decisions made by the asylum-deciding state. Dublin sets out criteria for returning asylum-seekers to the country with jurisdiction for the asylum decision and provides for information-sharing with the responsible state. The conditions for actually granting refugee status remain the responsibility of each country.

The goal is to prevent asylum-shopping and multiple claims by limiting the circumstances for deciding applications within the EC, among applicants and countries alike. This worthy objective may be difficult to achieve in practice, however, because of the "in transit" issue.

The responsibility of a state to examine a case can be triggered even when the asylum-seeker may simply have passed through an airport enroute to his destination. Thus, there is the potential for one state to examine a claim, determine it is not the deciding state, send the claimant onward, receive the claimant back if the next state determines it is not the deciding state, etc. Such shuttling of cases is further complicated by the Convention's requirement to examine cases rather than to decide them. There is no binding requirement for any state to decide.

Interstate disputes of this nature are probably inevitable, but can be avoided if signatories are judicious in their implementation of the Convention. Problems are likely to be ameliorated if substantive agreement can be reached over time on the legal standards and interpretations to be used to decide asylum cases. Such efforts are already underway as a function of Maastricht Treaty processes.

The Draft External Borders Convention is an extension of the essential provisions of the Schengen Convention to cover all twelve EC members. Legally, it would prevail over the provisions of Schengen if there are discrepancies. Adoption of the Convention by EC states has been delayed by a dispute over its application in Gibraltar between Great Britain and Spain.

The Convention stipulates entry requirements for non-EC nationals and places critical aspects of immigration regulation, particularly visa issuance criteria, on a European footing. It establishes a common European visa that is valid for three months. It also allows non-EC nationals residing in member states to move freely—a major breakthrough—though not to work or take up residence in other member states for up to three months. The Convention establishes sanctions for unlawful crossing of external borders and improper transport of passengers by carriers. It envisions automated information systems designating inadmissible persons.

b. The Maastricht Treaty on European Union
Incorporating provisions that have begun the process of harmonizing substantive elements of migration policy, the Maastricht Treaty

represents the most significant broadening of European integration goals since the Single Act. Adopted in December 1991, Maastricht brings an aspect of immigration policy into the ambit of Community competence for the first time.[69] Thus, EC bodies and decisions are to guide the adoption of measures to determine visa policy matters, including the list of countries from which EC nations will require visas.

Other aspects of migration policy harmonization are to be treated as intergovernmental matters. That is, they will be the province of Justice and Home Affairs ministries, who are to coordinate and cooperate outside the framework of Community law but operate under the general oversight of the European Council. Their work is to address nine specific topics, including asylum, external borders, and immigration policy.[70]

This third pillar of the Maastricht Treaty institutionalizes the *sui generis* cooperation which led to common positions on a range of matters including family reunion, manifestly unfounded asylum claims that trigger accelerated processing, and safe countries for return of asylum-seekers.[71] Examples of the range of issues being taken up in the intergovernmental process are admission of students, combating illegal employment, principles of expulsion, labor migration, information programs and training contracts for East Europeans and North Africans, and harmonizing substantive aspects of asylum law.

Furthermore, basic principles have been set forth in the communiqué from the Edinburgh Summit, which met in December 1992. The European Council's Declaration on Principles of Governing External Aspects of Migration Policy (see Appendix B) represents the first comprehensive policy statement toward international migration that has been made by senior European leaders.

It recognizes the destabilizing potential of uncontrolled immigration; cites improved human rights, democracy and economic conditions as required to reduce migration; and sees the need for coordination of foreign policy, economic cooperation and immigration and asylum policy in addressing migration movements. This statement of philosophy and the framework provided by the European Union Treaty constitute a solid base on which to build future policy.

It remains to be seen how effective this extensive legal framework will be and how quickly European states will move to put it into actual practice. To date, the Schengen Convention has been ratified by eight signatory states[72] and the Dublin Convention has been ratified by five EC member countries.[73] The External Borders Convention has not been signed.

Nevertheless, the many structures and policies that are evolving represent an impressive record of achievement. In combination, they constitute the principal elements of an immigration system. Nations' immigration systems consist of explicit practices and mechanisms to effect visa issuance; border controls; admission of immigrants and their family members and of refugees and asylum-seekers; workplace regulation; legal and naturalization rights of non-citizens; and expulsion procedures. The policies that govern these functions and the functions themselves are now all at varying stages of being established among European Community countries. All these policies must lead to fully integrating non-EC citizens who legally reside in member countries. Effective integration is indispensable to a nation's ability to obtain public acceptance of immigration.[74]

With the contours of an immigration system now apparent, the questions become the following: What will European immigration policy look like when it is actually implemented? Can Europe successfully achieve a common policy and become an immigration region?

C. EUROPE AND IMMIGRATION TOMORROW

With the generalized uncertainty about the future that is pervading Europe and the growing intolerance and public disapproval foreigners are experiencing, it is difficult to imagine how the concepts sketched above will work in actual practice. Despite the progress that has been made, formidable obstacles remain.

The primary obstacle is the distance between European policy development processes on immigration questions and public opinion. As political leaders assert that Europe is not an immigration region, regional organizations have constructed a full-fledged immigration system. The absence of transparency—although Maastricht is a step toward greater openness—is analogous to the claim made throughout Europe that the end of guestworker programs in the early 1970s closed off foreigner inflows. In fact, most European states have maintained active admissions programs for family members of resident foreigners, the mainstay of immigrant admissions schemes.

If Europe is to succeed in overcoming the obstacles that it faces on the immigration front, these key aspects must be addressed:

1. A Closed Debate

The delays in ratification of the critical conventions may not be unrelated to the lack of openness and public discussion surrounding the development and adoption of measures to address immigration and asylum questions. Officials of member states have not invited broad consideration of measures that will have profound effects on daily life and about which public opinion must be better informed and more fully considered.

Both the Dublin and External Borders Conventions were negotiated and drafted through closed-door processes. The Ad Hoc Immigration Group which produced them is now responsible for formulating harmonized immigration policies.[75] The documents and agendas for its work are treated as confidential. Because the processes are intergovernmental, rather than within the competence of the Community, deliberations and decisions are not subject to parliamentary review or EC judicial procedures and institutions.

The result is not only that opportunities are being lost to build public understanding and encourage informed debate, but suspicion is widespread among interested parties about the consequences of new policies. Civil libertarians believe that information systems listing inadmissible persons will violate individual rights; refugee advocates fear that asylum rights will be eroded, jeopardizing important refugee-protection principles; and non-white EC nationals worry that they will suffer new forms of discrimination as a byproduct of strengthened immigration control measures.

Whether or not such concerns are legitimate cannot be evaluated, precisely because of the dearth of open debate. This closed policy-making style seriously jeopardizes the success of the entire enterprise, and contributes to Europe's democracy deficit.

2. The Plethora of Forums

Immigration matters are now treated in at least 30 official European forums. Not only is the schedule of meetings constant, there is little coordination among the various groups nor the political strength that is needed to move a complex agenda forward. To some extent, the plethora of forums has grown out of political necessity, because governments had to be seen to be doing something. Thus, a number of parallel processes are underway.[76] However, those reactions do not per se create a policy. Consolidation is now necessary.

Several circles are needed, so that both a special Community-wide forum and a broader forum exist where migration matters are a basic concern. The best evolution in this regard would be for EC processes and institutions to become the primary European setting for immigration policy development and implementation. This would place immigration squarely into the framework where overarching issues of regional concern are handled. It would also overcome the deficiencies of the intergovernmental process, which include the inability to compel states to bring national laws into conformity with Community policy and the democratic deficit.

In this connection, the Maastricht right of co-initiative should be fully utilized: the EC Commission should present an annual migration report to the European Parliament and Council that includes proposals for action. This presentation should be made by the Commissioner for Immigration and Asylum Issues, who would be Europe's de facto High Commissioner for Migrants. Furthermore, EC institutions should work closely and cooperatively with the United Nations High Commissioner for Refugees (UNHCR).

The Conference on Security and Cooperation in Europe (CSCE), which has begun to take up migration, offers unique attributes as the key broader grouping of nations. In addition to including Western European states that are not Community nations, it engages the East. Its consensus procedures are cumbersome, but it is the best political forum for conflict-prevention and for bringing former bloc nations and Russia into processes for problem-solving on migration issues. Thus, it places migration into a context where it can be properly treated as both a cause and result of political instability, and CSCE conflict-prevention processes can be directed toward migration prevention purposes. Such efforts can be importantly augmented by the Council of Europe which is taking up migration questions and will consider increased protection for minorities through the European Court of Human Rights at its Vienna summit meeting in October 1994.

Finally, migration has been a portfolio within the Organization for Economic Cooperation and Development (OECD) long before the issues became frontline political concerns. Its analytic and information exchange efforts among industrialized nations are invaluable and should be strengthened and broadened. The interrelationship of migration and population issues was also addressed at the March 1993 European preparatory conference for the United Nations Population Conference in Cairo in 1994. Such broad-based consideration of the issues is essential for establishing new points of international consensus and action.

3. Fortress Europe

Just as Communist barriers fell that kept people in, the West is accused of erecting new walls to keep newly freed peoples out. Establishing immigration systems and policies in Europe should be the path to effective facilitation and regulation of migration flows that are inevitable, and to incorporating immigration effectively into nations' economic and social goals. Nevertheless, Fortress Europe could also be the outcome if policy implementation is not generous and is driven by xenophobia.

Europe's response to displaced persons from ex-Yugoslavia represents a worrisome case. The overwhelming majority of persons displaced by the fighting and violence remain within their republics or nearby. However, those who needed to get to Western Europe have been subjected to stringent visa requirements and an attitude that they are not refugees and would simply swell overloaded asylum rolls if admitted. The Yugoslavian war is a classic example of why first asylum principles exist and must be upheld. Moreover, ex-Yugoslavia's victims of ethnic cleansing are classic examples of persons subject to persecution because of religion or national origin, the grounds set forth in international refugee instruments as the grounds for treatment as a refugee.

Narrow, rigidly construed implementation of immigration precepts will be especially damaging where the asylum convention is concerned. If states are too literal in their interpretation of the "in transit" provisions of a common asylum policy, there is the risk not only of not moving decisions forward swiftly, but of serious disputes between neighboring states about responsibility for cases or groups. Thus, countries like Germany and Italy within the Community, and others such as Austria and Sweden, could be subject to disproportionate burdens.

Similarly, the idea of "safe countries" that is becoming embodied in asylum doctrine could have serious repercussions for Eastern European states. If Western European nations do not generously interpret asylum law, large numbers of denied asylum seekers could be returned to now-safe Eastern European states through which the applicants traveled enroute from Romania, the FSU, or elsewhere.

In this regard, Germany has just concluded an agreement with Poland under which Poland agrees to receive asylum-seekers who use Poland to come to Germany.[77] Yet Poland has no capacity nor experience in adjudicating refugee claims and will have maintenance burdens for large numbers with far fewer resources to apply. The agreement provides for financial assistance to Poland (DM 120 million in 1993-94). Nonetheless, the prospect of Western European nations responding to domestic political pressures by relocating portions of their asylum populations in this manner (a similar Czech-German agreement is under discussion) could have grave consequences for states that are not yet in a position to object but have fragile economies and democracies. And although the former Communist bloc states may now be safe, serious questions remain about whether they can provide adequate protection for those refugees within the asylum pool who need it.

Fortress Europe tendencies will also hurt intra-EC burden-sharing if new emergencies erupt. One such scenario concerns Albania. Current estimates are that within the year, there will be so little food in Albania that malnutrition could become widespread. A large "boat people" flow to Italy could ensue. Should Italy be individually responsible if this occurs? At present, there is no mechanism or discussion aimed at handling such eventualities collectively, efforts to fashion a common immigration policy notwithstanding. Emergencies will occur and deeply restrictionist attitudes will undermine Europe's ability to share burdens when needed.

Evidence that argues against the fear of a Fortress Europe is also strong. In fact, very large numbers of non-Europeans now reside in European Community countries, and wholesale expulsions have not occurred, despite anti-foreigner impulses. Although there are difficulties, countries like Germany are handling a substantial immigration population that consists of ethnic Germans, asylum-seekers, and other foreigners Germany has received. Germany's commitment to receive its "Aussiedler" population (ethnic Germans from Eastern Europe and the FSU) is not described as immigration but it is, in fact, immigration, whatever the label.

Germany has also, as part of its inter-party agreement on Constitutional changes to address asylum, proposed a comprehensive immigration policy somewhat analogous to the quota system used by the United States. Its objectives are to continue admitting family members of legal residents; host a quota of "war refugees," to be determined in consultation with state government officials, as long as the conflict persists; pace the entry of Aussiedler admissions by receiving no more than ten percent of the previous year's Aussiedler number;[78] and authorize temporary labor contracts for up to 100,000 workers annually.

The agreement also eases citizenship barriers for some longtime foreign residents. In the aftermath of the Solingen crisis, Chancellor Kohl has said he will soon ease tight citizenship restrictions on young German-born Turks and favors reconsideration of Germany's citizenship law.[79] These are important psychological steps, showing new flexibility in Germany's traditional view that the nation is bound by blood, not soil.[80]

Levels of admission, or quotas, for immigrants are also implicit in a draft Migration Convention that is being proposed by Austria for Europe. The draft sets forth a code of conduct and other pertinent standards to govern state behavior in the migration realm. The draft leaves many important questions unanswered, for example, how European admissions numbers would be allocated among countries.

But, should the idea of a quota system take hold, levels of annual immigrant admissions could be proposed by the EC Commission, after consultation with the European Parliament, to the EC Council of Ministers. Or, the EC could establish a new position of High Commissioner for Immigration, with duties that would include making recommendations for meeting the EC's immigration needs. Such recommendations would be based on professional and labor requirements, family unification and other needs determined by member countries. Asylum-seekers would be outside the purview of annual quotas. A Migration Convention might also allow for a non-EC national legally residing in a member state to work in another EC country, thereby increasing the labor pool within the EC able to respond to the region's labor demands.

Such developments are important counterpoints to Fortress Europe. They suggest that an understanding is developing of the positive role immigration can play. Immigration controls and disciplined procedures for managing migration flows are legitimate and necessary. But they must be combined with a generous interpretation of refugee and asylum obligations and various methods for admitting reasonable numbers of new immigrants, for family unity and labor market purposes, if a common policy is to succeed.

*   *   *

Urgent new migration pressures from the East and growing pressures from the South have combined with an asylum crisis and anti-foreigner violence to propel immigration to the top of the political agenda in Europe. Having struggled unsuccessfully to mount unilateral solutions, individual states are progressively looking to European institutions and processes to shape responses and a common policy. As a result, migration is becoming a major new arena of Europe-wide policy-making. At the same time, the difficulty of relinquishing sovereignty over this core attribute of the traditional nation-state has created highly disparate decision processes. Unless they are rapidly consolidated in favor of Community, rather than intergovernmental, policy-making processes, promising new initiatives could unravel.

European officials and organs seem to have adopted the notion of Europe as an immigration region and have moved aggressively to design workable immigration systems. Their vision, however, diverges sharply from public perceptions about immigrants, which are too often shaped by anti-foreigner voices that go unchallenged. This is a dangerous abyss that could lead to highly restrictive practices, forced by xenophobia. Such an outcome would be corrosive to Europe's economic well-being, inter-state relations, and global influence, as well as to its self-image of centuries-long openness to the broader world.

IV. Japan

Japan's historical experience on migration matters is completely different from that of either North America or Europe. Although Japan did have some emigration before and immediately after World War II, when Japanese settled in Hawaii, the West Coast of the United States, Latin America, Southeast Asia and Manchuria, emigration did not shape modern Japan as it did Europe. And immigration has also not played a role in the life of this densely populated island nation. With a population of foreigners of just one percent,[81] one of Japan's most distinctive national characteristics is ethnic homogeneity.

The Southeast Asian refugee crisis of the 1970s led Japan to attempt resettlement of a handful of Vietnamese boat people, and the arrival in 1989 of 3,000 Chinese, disguised as political refugees from Vietnam, triggered fears of abusive asylum claims and fueled Japan's perpetual anxiety about the migration consequences of political or economic instability in its giant neighbor. Nonetheless, Japan's island location and policies have left it largely untouched by the migration events of recent years that have affected other advanced industrial nations in dramatic ways.

However, even in Japan, the picture is beginning to change. Migration issues are forcing their way onto the national agenda for economic reasons. The nexus between demography and economic growth is causing Japan to look abroad for labor. Labor migration is by no means a major public issue and the influence of foreign workers upon labor markets remains very small. But Japan's departure from tradition in this realm is significant and represents a revealing point of convergence with other Trilateral nations.

A. LABOR SHORTAGES AND FOREIGN WORKERS

In 1992, Japan introduced a foreign worker trainee program intended to provide badly needed labor to certain Japanese employers while also giving training and experience to workers from less developed countries. The program was recommended to the Prime Minister in December 1991 by a subcommittee of the Provisional Committee for

Promotion of Administrative Reform.[82] The proposal tried to allow for the entry of more foreign workers than provided in current legislation, which permits only skilled workers. The concept is that of an on-the-job training system whereby employers would also be responsible for medical care and other benefits.

The intent is to train about 100,000 foreigners a year. Four leading government ministries jointly have set up a body called the Japan International Training Cooperation Organization (JITCO) to unify government and business training efforts. Members can request trainees through JITCO which is to act as a liaison between foreign countries and member companies and groups.

A key element of the program is to establish training centers in particular sending nations. They are not only to select migrants but also to give brief instruction in elementary industrial production techniques and Japanese language and customs. Workers would then work in Japan for two-year periods and be rotated back to their home countries. Upon return, the training centers would, presumably, also perform a labor-placement and exchange role.[83]

1. The Demographic Imperative

The trainee program is the government's response to an intense internal debate about growing labor shortages and calls from employers for help. Japan is at a crucial demographic and labor force crossroads which has profound economic implications for its future. Fertility declined very sharply after World War II and has been below replacement level for decades. Ageing is occurring more quickly than in any other advanced industrial society. An inverted age pyramid is likely by the end of the next generation, with significantly smaller numbers of labor force entrants by the end of the decade.

The effects of these trends are already apparent. Unemployment is about two percent, which is considered full employment. With the recent severe slump, this situation has loosened somewhat. Some workers have been dismissed, especially illegal workers, and the discussion of labor shortages has abated. But the projections do not change: worker deficits are likely to reach one million by the turn of the century,[84] almost half of them in key economic sectors, such as the computer industry. With aggressive automation and "out-sourcing" schemes, the deficit can be halved at best.[85]

At the same time, Japan does not suffer from an absolute shortage of labor. Unemployment rates among its oldest workers are substantial, and overemployment is widespread because of the tradition of life-long employment arrangements. The labor force participation rates of women stand at considerably less than those for most other advanced industrial societies. Furthermore, the deployment of mostly female workers in entry-level service industry jobs is remarkably wasteful by Western standards. Japan's low-level service personnel, for example, outnumber that of comparable U.S. establishments by a factor of about four.

But the social forces required to address these mismatches are not in evidence. Surpluses of workers in the countryside are loathe to move to cities where the labor force needs exist. The culture mitigates against making aggressive efforts to upgrade the economic role of women.

The apparent unwillingness of the government to devise a long-term labor market strategy is quite opposite from its stance in the late 1960s, when the economy was booming and industries demanded they be allowed to hire foreigners to meet labor needs. The government refused, instituting policies that restructured domestic workforces and contributed to longer-term competitiveness.

Today, in the absence of readily available labor, small to medium-size firms are suffering the most. The pinch is particularly acute in metal-processing, construction, and the service sector. In 1991, the Japan Food Service Association proposed admission of 600,000 foreign workers, a number equivalent to one percent of the work force. "This issue will affect the very existence of our labor-intensive industries," said one Association member.[86]

Such pleas are inevitably exaggerated and would not be made in today's recession environment. Nonetheless, Japanese, especially younger workers, increasingly reject the three D's—difficult, dirty and dangerous jobs.[87] They prefer the large companies that offer lifetime employment and generous benefits.

2. Illegal Workers

The employment of illegal workers has, therefore, sharply risen, particularly in blue-collar and low-level service jobs. Estimates of the size of the illegal population show steady increases, from 160,000 in 1991 to 278,000 by mid-1992.[88] This is a dramatic increase, however, over a few tens of thousands just three years ago. Another revealing measure is a 75 percent increase in the incidence of visa overstays between 1991 and 1992 and a 95 percent increase in the number of foreigners who were refused entry between 1990 and 1991. The largest group refused was from Iran, followed by Thailand and Malaysia.[89] Other countries whose nationals make up Japan's illegal population include Bangladesh, China, Pakistan, the Philippines and South Korea.

The illegal population originally came to Japan as tourists, students, or entertainers. In addition, Japan had bilateral agreements with Bangladesh, Iran and Pakistan to encourage commerce and travel. The agreements permitted travel without visas. Although they have now been suspended, many of the travelers that were admitted stayed, becoming the predominant cheap labor force in Japan.

Cross-national worker migration is widespread throughout Asia, and with 11.82 million people from Asian countries having worked in other nations over the past 20 years, the numbers are sizeable.[90] Because there are substantial gaps in living standards between Japan and many neighboring lands, illegal migration should not be surprising or unexpected. In one week's work at a construction job in Japan, for example, a Pakistani university graduate can earn the equivalent of one year's wages at home.[91]

Nonetheless, illegal workers are a new phenomenon because of the lack of cultural and ethnic links with other nations and the antipathy of the Japanese population to foreigners. The same issues and problems that have become familiar dilemmas in other advanced industrial societies are now arising in Japan.

- Workers' rights are regularly violated, with the most common being non-payment of wages.

- Illegal workers are not covered by work-related accident or health insurance and cannot receive medical treatment through the public health system. Employment-related injuries, which occur regularly because illegals do the hardest, most dangerous work, have led to serious illness and even death because they go untreated.

- Workers frequently must work 11 or more hours per day and are denied the required minimum 25 percent additional pay for overtime. With recession, they are readily dismissed.

- Workers are denied paid holidays and do not receive semiannual bonuses given to company employees.

- Illegal female workers are sometimes forced into prostitution.

- "Employment brokers" take advantage of workers' illegal status.

All these characteristics of illegal employment give employers in marginal or labor-intensive industries a crucial competitive edge, allowing many to survive and even thrive who would otherwise be likely to go out of business.

3. Government Policy

In June 1990, a new law went into effect that (a) established penalties for employers for the first time for hiring illegal workers; (b) liberalized opportunities for the admission of skilled foreign workers, while prohibiting the entry of unskilled workers; and (c) permitted employment rights and residence for foreigners of Japanese origin. This final provision essentially applied to Latin Americans with Japanese ancestry. Inviting their return represented an effort to introduce a new, unskilled work force that was imagined to be culturally compatible.[92] More than 150,000 have taken advantage of the Japanese-origin provisions.

Because the law prohibits admission of unskilled workers, the government's foreign worker program has been explained not as a guestworker program but as an effort to achieve training and development goals for labor-source countries. Trainees, who have been mainly from China, Thailand, South Korea, Malaysia and the Philippines, are said to be the basis for technology transfer and the costs are being taken from development assistance funds. Although disingenuous, this formulation resolves a set of political problems.

- Importing unskilled workers is prohibited by the immigration law, but trainees are not workers.

- Consistent with the labor migration tradition of the region, India, Thailand and the Philippines have been exerting pressure on Japan to establish worker programs. Saying no and maintaining good relations was becoming increasingly difficult.

- Japan was censured by the United Nations Human Rights Commission for abuses of illegal workers and some citizens groups within the country have begun to take up their cause. Providing an alternative, above-board labor supply of foreign workers for which fair compensation and benefits are provided was seen as urgent for Japan's public image at home and abroad.

The new trainee policy has sparked the classic economic debate. Those who favor it argue that accepting workers contributes to the economic growth of developing nations, contributes to growth in the domestic economy, and provides alternatives to illegal workers. Those who oppose it ask whether worker programs are the best way to achieve development; remind that growth can only be sustained over the long term through fair competition and technological advances, innovation and a highly skilled and trained work force; and question whether Japan can solve problems of social friction with resident foreign populations.

Nomenclature notwithstanding, Japan's steps towards adopting the guestworker model to confront its demographic destiny have all the earmarks of the European experience of the 1960s and '70s. That experience is, in the words of Max Frisch, a Swiss writer, "We asked for workers, but people came." The signs are already apparent.

- The need for cross-cultural training of Japanese working with Chinese workers on production lines has arisen.

- Schools are being confronted for the first time with children whose first language is not Japanese and need bilingual instruction.

- Concerns are being voiced that Japan's relations with developing countries in the region could suffer if it treats Asian workers as an expendable commodity.

- Labor unions now have some non-Japanese members whom they see as ripe for protection, given the harsh conditions under which many work.

At the same time, recent polls report that only two percent of the population thinks the rapid rise of foreign workers will turn Japan into a multi-racial society or that there will be a greater willingness to accept foreign labor.[93] There appears to be a serious gap developing between public expectations and the longer-term implications of seemingly innocuous government actions.

Neither the government nor employers seem inclined to rationalize the labor force or restructure low-wage labor markets to overcome the demographic deficit. Japan's choices are to accept lower growth, robotize even further, tap the dormant female work force, or introduce foreign workers. Lower growth has never been an acceptable alternative for Japan. There are limits to the use of robots since they cannot solve many of the labor shortage problems of service sectors. So, the likely directions are greater female labor force participation and foreign workers.

Introducing foreign labor without systematically preparing the public for the significant consequences it may have for Japanese life could invite serious social and cultural antagonisms. On the other hand, Japan may be able to contain the broader social effects of guestworker programs by carefully segregating work among Japanese and foreigners and by imposing tight limits (such as the prohibition on accompanying family members) on the latitude given to foreign workers while in Japan.

Albeit limited in scope, the journey on which Japan seems to be embarked presents the developed world with one of the more remarkable migration policy experiments underway in any Trilateral country today.

B. JAPAN'S INTERNATIONAL ROLE

Although not a refugee resettlement country, Japan has become increasingly active and engaged in some aspects of the international refugee agenda. It has defined its role as primarily one of providing financial support for humanitarian activities. Since the era of the Vietnamese boatlifts, Japan has been increasing contributions to the United Nations High Commissioner for Refugees (UNHCR), and it is now among the top donors, contributing over $100 million annually.

That commitment has been augmented by the appointment of Sadako Ogata to the position of United Nations High Commissioner for Refugees, one of the first Japanese to head a major UN agency. In addition, Japan has assumed responsibility for a substantial share of the costs of financing international support for the Cambodian peace plan.

Japan's long-term business strategies have targeted substantial investment to neighboring Asian states. This serves Japan's economic interests but also has the derivative effect of significant job creation in nearby countries with excess labor supplies. Where China is concerned, the specter of migrations as a byproduct of instability has led Japan to pursue policies of economic linkage and development of coastal areas nearest Japan. Its reluctance to associate itself with criticism of China's democracy or human rights record is a pragmatic expression of national interests flowing from geopolitical verities.

Nevertheless, in a world where global issues are increasingly posing complex political and cultural pressures, it may not be possible for Japan to limit its role to "checkbook diplomacy." As it grapples with the demands of being a world power, it too may be unable to remain impervious to the domestic transformations that international migration pressures bring in their wake. For this reason, the seemingly narrow issue of foreign workers has potentially profound implications for Japanese life and society.

V. The International Community and Refugees: Different Contexts, Changing Approaches

From the standpoint of international law and practice, regulating migration processes is recognized to be a sovereign right and prerogative of individual states. In December 1990, the UN General Assembly adopted a new instrument known as the International Convention on the Protection of the Rights of All Migrant Workers and Members of Their Families. Ten years in negotiation, it speaks to the growing significance of international migration and the need to establish international legal norms to guide the behavior of states in responding to it. However, the Convention has not been ratified nor are there international agencies charged with responsibility for making it operational.[94]

The only superseding international instrument where migration matters are concerned is the 1951 Convention Relating to the Status of Refugees. The Convention binds signatories to observe the right of first asylum and the principle of *non-refoulement*, i.e. non-return of refugees to a country where they have been or might be subject to persecution on account of race, religion, nationality, political opinion or membership in a social group. The Convention and its 1967 Protocol (see Appendix C) have 116 state signatories.

Implementing the Convention is the responsibility of the United Nations High Commissioner for Refugees (UNHCR), an agency of the UN which was established at the time the Convention was adopted. Because the most dynamic aspect of international action today on refugee and migration matters surrounds the activities of UNHCR and the use of the refugee convention, this chapter concentrates on outlining those developments.

When UNHCR was established, the refugee problem was the massive displacement of people from Eastern Europe, fleeing newly Communist regimes. UNHCR assistance concentrated on legal, technical measures to help exiles navigate entry and documentation requirements, mostly in Western Europe.

The locus of refugee dislocations has changed in the intervening years and with it the political and strategic considerations surrounding the international humanitarian response. This has been reflected in the methods UNHCR has devised to carry out its mandate and the demands that have been placed upon it by the international community.

In the 1960s and into the 1970s, decolonization in Africa led to flight generated by violence, rather than targeted persecution as it was manifested in Europe. Neighboring countries became host to large displaced populations and the international community provided support through the UN and a wide array of non-governmental organizations (NGOs) to ease the burden of hosting sizeable refugee populations until they returned to newly formed states.

During this period another, broader definition of a refugee was introduced to take into account the different circumstances that had arisen in Africa. In its 1969 Convention Governing the Specific Aspects of Refugee Problems, the Organization of African Unity (OAU) described a refugee as someone fleeing war, violence and serious public disorder. A similar formulation was subsequently adopted by Latin American nations in their Cartagena Declaration.

These broader definitions have not been recognized by the developed nations for purposes of refugee resettlement. However, they are accepted by UNHCR for purposes of providing relief and assistance. Two sets of law and practice have developed, therefore, with the broader definition characterizing actual practice and experience in most parts of the world where sizeable refugee populations are now found.

The wars fueled by superpower rivalries created a third shift during the 1970s and 1980s. Not only was UNHCR called upon to operate long-term care and assistance programs in camps, some for more than a decade, but the duration of the wars and the unlikely prospects for return within any foreseeable period led to substantial permanent refugee resettlement in third countries outside the regions of the conflicts.

The end of the Cold War has ushered in a fourth period. Conflict within countries and regions is along ethnic and religious lines, leading to massive internal displacement of populations and the destruction of the state itself in some cases. Generous refugee resettlement by third countries is no longer politically attractive nor consistent with broader strategic objectives, so humanitarian relief has begun to concentrate on care-in-place and be accompanied by political initiatives to defuse the conflicts themselves.

These new dangers exist as the end of the Cold War has awakened long-dormant opportunities for refugee populations to repatriate and for the UN system to address obstacles to peace, as envisioned by its founders. As Sadako Ogata, the High Commissioner for Refugees, has said, today's refugee dilemmas must be understood against a "complex background of hope and hazard."

It is within this context that new international standards and norms are emerging and being tested. The ways in which states and the international community are grappling with recent refugee crises provide revealing insights into the international responses to humanitarian emergencies that are evolving for the future.

A. THE AFTERMATH OF THE GULF WAR

The spring 1991 exodus of hundreds of thousands of Kurds into the inhospitable mountains of northern Iraq at the end of the Gulf War was the most explosive refugee emergency that has occurred since organized, international protection efforts were established. In three weeks, 1.7 million Kurds fled their homes.[95] Six weeks later, most had been returned, the result of equally unprecedented events.

The Refugee Convention binds neighboring states to providing first asylum in the face of refugee outflows. But in this case, the numbers of people were so overwhelming and sensitivity about an indigenous Kurdish separatist movement ran so high that Turkey closed the border and refused to provide asylum.[96] A standoff ensued during which many died from exposure, especially infants and children, while the international press recorded in vivid detail the plight of hundreds of thousands of people caught between Iraqi aggression and Turkish intransigence.

As a NATO member and indispensable partner in the Gulf War coalition, Turkey's decision was immutable. Some other solution had to be devised to respond to mounting political pressure. Thus was born Resolution 688 (see Appendix D), the Security Council decision that (a) held that Iraq's actions to repress its citizens, forcing them to become refugees and displaced persons, constituted a threat to international peace and security, and (b) authorized immediate access by international humanitarian organizations to those in Iraq needing assistance. For the first time, the consequences of a refugee crisis were designated a political threat that called for political countermeasures. The international community had taken the unprecedented act of authorizing humanitarian intervention.

Operation Provide Comfort followed, in which the massive military resources in the region that had been used to fight the war were applied to the humanitarian mission of bringing the displaced population down from the mountains to safety zones that were established north of the 36th parallel. The UNHCR and other civilian UN agencies then took over, providing assistance and protection to the Kurds in Iraq.

The UNHCR's protection mandate is limited to serving persons who have crossed international borders. There are sound reasons for this delineation. It establishes the conditions for the safety of refugee relief operations and of relief workers. And it allows for cooperation from the sovereign state without which relief cannot be delivered effectively.

A mission calling for protection to be provided *within* the country in which the refugee is in danger was entirely new. It caused, in the words of one observer, virtually a theological debate within UNHCR and the humanitarian community about the parameters of refugee assistance and doctrine. Ultimately, the authority for UNHCR's work in Iraq was based not on Resolution 688, but on a separate Memorandum of Understanding negotiated with Iraqi authorities precisely to resolve the contradiction between UNHCR's mandate and the special circumstances of the Iraqi case.

The new themes that emerged in the Kurdish case include the following:

- As a matter of international principle, massive refugee displacements have been defined as a threat to international peace and security, establishing a justification for intervention for humanitarian purposes that supersedes national sovereignty.

- Military forces were used to perform civilian relief functions in the absence of any other sufficient capability to respond to a massive emergency.

- Safety zones can be a pragmatic alternative to first asylum, but they cannot be established without the acquiescence of state authorities, if they are to be viable from a protection standpoint.

Although laced with "firsts," the degree to which the Kurdish case actually established precedents that will be applied elsewhere remains to be seen. The coalition-driven war combined with the ready availability of massive military resources may have provided a unique set of circumstances. Nevertheless, the very idea that new principles of international humanitarian response can be established seems, at a minimum, to be serving as an enduring legacy and provided the foundation for subsequent international action in Somalia to deliver food and restore order.

B. CAMBODIA

With the signing of the Paris Peace Agreement in October 1991, the way finally became clear to repatriate 360,000 refugees who had lived on the Thai-Cambodian border for more than 12 years. Returns began in spring 1992, organized and supervised by the UNHCR as part of the international community's peacemaking mechanism, the UN Transitional Authority in Cambodia (UNTAC). All had voluntarily returned in time for elections in May 1993, as called for in the Paris accords.

The effort to return peace, facilitate reconciliation, and promote democratic processes in Cambodia is one example of conflict resolution that was made possible by a new atmosphere of international cooperation and a revitalized UN taking on a new generation of peace initiatives. Traditionally, refugee doctrine has adhered to three durable solutions for refugees: repatriation, local integration in the country of first asylum, or resettlement in third countries. While repatriation has always been the preferred solution, the Cold War rendered it all but impossible in practice.

UNHCR-supervised repatriations in Central America predated the Cambodian operation and are underway in other parts of the world as well. Altogether, 1.5 million refugees returned to their home countries in 1992 alone.[97] Moreover, there are about twenty additional cases where sizeable repatriations have begun or will be possible in the near future. They include Eritrea, Afghanistan and Mozambique.

The Cambodian operation represents the most difficult and arguably the most significant because it is inextricably linked with the most intense, comprehensive effort to date to facilitate peace in a deeply damaged country. As such, repatriation is an integral part of the peace process and an important test of the role humanitarian initiatives can play in achieving bold, new political objectives.

UNHCR's work in Cambodia has included repairing roads to make returnee routes passable, upgrading rail transportation, digging wells, and de-mining fields for farming. Adjustments to its plans have had to be made along the way. For example, assistance packages were to include housing and land, a promise that became impossible to meet. Cash grants were substituted instead.

In addition to transportation and reception assistance, UNHCR has provided short-term project funding, for anything from seed production to manufacture of artificial limbs, intended to serve as a stopgap while lengthier development assistance planning efforts are underway. In these ways, UNHCR is contributing to recovery and has tried to serve as a catalyst for effective reconstruction by bridging the gap between relief and development.

At the same time, there is no consensus on where repatriation ends and reintegration/development begins. UNHCR has interpreted its repatriation assignment in Cambodia in exceptionally broad terms. But it is understandably reluctant to undertake responsibilities that go even further beyond its expertise, or require sustained institutional commitments. Development aid pledges of $880 million have been made for Cambodia, a substantial commitment of resources. The difficulty now is putting them to effective use beyond the quick impact project funding UNHCR has introduced.

How far does UNHCR's responsibility extend once refugees return home? At what point do former refugees become ordinary citizens? These are questions that have never been satisfactorily resolved within UNHCR, nor addressed by UN member states. No longer theoretical, they are now crucial policy and operational matters that must be answered for repatriation initiatives to succeed. If the answers call for UNHCR to become more fully involved in reintegration activities beyond repatriation, more resources, new forms of institutional expertise, and an expanded mandate would be needed.[98]

As peace and development efforts are mounted in Cambodia and other countries emerging from protracted armed conflicts, they must help the entire population, not only repatriated refugees. The extent to which the development challenge is met will ultimately be the test of whether today's refugee crises are resolved in the long term. This is particularly the case in the many repatriation situations where international organizations are not the prime movers, but where refugees repatriate themselves, unassisted and often unnoticed.

Most repatriation, in fact, is refugee-induced and occurs under conditions of conflict where the political difficulties that generated flight in the first place have not changed. Thus, the dangers have not abated, but the choices facing the refugee are so hopeless (two-thirds of today's refugees are the products of conflicts more than ten years old) that he gives up on asylum and takes his chances with return. Millions more have returned home than are captured by official statistics, because more than 90 percent of actual repatriations have been irregular, taking place without formal assistance or by means of a structured program.[99]

But even where the international community is fully involved, the path to peace is precarious. The UNTAC initiative hung in the balance when Khmer Rouge forces refused to abide by the disarmament provisions of the peace accord and massacred Vietnamese civilians in a Southeast Asian version of ethnic cleansing. As the elections drew near, government forces began intimidating opposition party members through violent attacks that killed people and destroyed property. The Khmer Rouge turned to terror tactics, too, threatening to sabotage the voting itself. However, the sheer will of the Cambodian people to vote for peace, bolstered by the continuing presence of a neutral international force, prevailed and resulted in Cambodia's first truly democratic elections.

Difficult tests of the election surely lie ahead. As the UN peacekeeping presence recedes, its development programs must ascend in visibility and reach. Broad-based rural development initiatives—such as the health care, schools and potable water projects underway in the northwest region of the country where sizeable refugee repatriation occurred—can help counteract radical voices and government corruption. Such efforts by the international community are essential to securing the peace that Cambodians and the UNTAC effort have paid so dearly to win.

Thus, Cambodia has been and continues to serve as a laboratory for additional new refugee policy themes that include the following:

- Refugee repatriation has become an integral part of the UN's peacekeeping functions, and UNHCR is serving as a full participant in the international effort to bring peaceful solutions to countries of refugee origin.

- The most effective protection UNHCR can provide vulnerable populations, its physical presence, is proving to be as critical to effective repatriation as it has classically been when refugee emergencies first arise.

- Institutional and policy links between repatriation and reintegration/development activities must be effectively made if repatriation is to break the cycle of turmoil that leads to further refugee flight.

The dilemmas facing UNHCR where repatriations are concerned are inevitable, given its greatly expanded role in the wake of the Cold War. Successful repatriation in Cambodia has been especially important, for the stakes there are enormous. It has served as the first serious test of whether the opportunities opened up by the demise of superpower rivalries can indeed look to international bodies, relying on international law and democratic processes, to trace pathways to peace and stability.

C. EX-YUGOSLAVIA

Perhaps a dialectic is at work in the fact that refugee protection is being stretched to its limits in Europe, the place where it was born forty years ago. Furthermore, the paroxysm of violence that has seized ex-Yugoslavia has, as its very objective, to create refugees. Ethnic cleansing, as a political and military objective, is devoted to the proposition that populations must be permanently displaced.

Well before UN peacekeeping forces were deployed in Yugoslavia, UNHCR was asked to provide assistance, at first for displaced persons in Croatia (where four protected zones were created within the country). The hope was that giving humanitarian assistance as near as possible to the locus of conflict could limit and prevent further displacement. But the fighting spread to Bosnia-Herzegovina, and the Security Council called for and authorized the delivery of humanitarian aid to civilian victims there too. As the fighting intensified, Security Council resolutions steadily expanded the scope of humanitarian activity in Bosnia.

- The responsibilities of peacekeeping forces (UNPROFOR) were broadened to include protecting Sarajevo airport and access to the city, so that UNHCR could mount an airlift of supplies;

- Military force was authorized to insure delivery of humanitarian assistance; and

- UNPROFOR's mandate was broadened to include all of Bosnia for purposes of peacekeeping and support of UNHCR activities.

- Six "safe areas" have been created to which UN troops are to be deployed, so that humanitarian assistance can be supplied to besieged residents.

1. New Dilemmas

This escalation of the scope and responsibilities of UNHCR's work in ex-Yugoslavia, mandated by the Security Council, has again posed major dilemmas for the organization. The Convention definition of a refugee envisioned victims of ethnic cleansing as within the ambit of the concerns of UNHCR. But, just as with Iraq, the organization's traditional mandate limits its work to persons who have crossed international borders.[100]

Since the former regions of Yugoslavia are now autonomous states, the displaced from Serbia who were in Croatia, for example, were eligible to receive UNHCR attention. But by and large, the massive displacement has remained within the affected countries and demonstrates how artificial the international border limitation can sometimes be. The displaced, whether or not they have crossed an international border, are experiencing the same problems, created by the same conflict.

UNHCR's dilemma has been deepened by the need for military protection to enable it to protect and deliver relief supplies. This represents an historic departure for agencies whose effectiveness is anchored in a fierce devotion to neutrality and impartiality, so as to be able to work on all sides of political conflicts with strictly humanitarian aims as the objective. In contrast, the Security Council and its forces have distinctly political purposes. The danger is that linking these military forces to UNHCR's humanitarian duties could jeopardize and taint UNHCR's ability to operate with confidence among all relevant parties.

Nevertheless, conditions on the ground dictated the outcome. Humanitarian assistance could not be delivered in the absence of security. The linkage between humanitarian aid and military cover had to be made, not only in ex-Yugoslavia but subsequently in Somalia. Accordingly, protected airlift operations and land convoys to Sarajevo and other besieged centers have become a hallmark of the Balkan conflagration.

Finally, ethnic cleansing as an objective of aggression has presented humanitarian agencies with agonizing choices. In attempting to protect people inside their countries and prevent displacement, persuading people to remain where they are poses fundamental dangers to life and liberty. But helping people to move facilitates ethnic cleansing. The humanitarian agencies have put the lives of civilians first, though it aids and abets ethnic cleansing. But they have also attempted, through contingency planning for eventual they have also attempted, through contingency planning for eventual return, to keep the idea of return alive, in an effort to help thwart ethnic cleansing over the longer term.[101]

2. New Realities

In the eyes of UNHCR, its work in ex-Yugoslavia brings it into a symbiotic relationship with political processes dedicated to finding peaceful solutions to the conflict. The organization is serving as the humanitarian arm of the UN's work in the region, attempting to prevent refugee flows. By containing displacement, it sees its humanitarian activity as making time and space available for political initiatives to bear fruit. To that end, agreements that have been negotiated among the warring parties to facilitate release of certain groups of detainees not only assist the most beleaguered victims but also can be seen as confidence-building measures.

Albeit courageous and perhaps visionary, humanitarianism has proven to be no match for deadly aggression. By UNHCR's own calculation (see Table 8), about three million people—refugees,

TABLE 8
Refugees and Displaced Persons in Ex-Yugoslavia

Present Location	from Croatia	from Bosnia-Herzegovina	Total
Croatia	246,000	283,000	561,000* (R)
UN Protected Areas (in Croatia)	87,000	—	87,000 (E)
Serbia	164,000	294,000	458,000 (R)
Bosnia-Herzegovina	70,000	740,000	810,000 (E)
Montenegro	7,000	58,000	65,000 (R)
Slovenia	n/a	n/a	40,000 (R)
Macedonia	3,000	29,000	32,000 (R)
TOTALS	**577,000**	**1,404,000**	**2,053,000†**

Source: UNHCR Office of the Special Envoy for former Yugoslavia, Zagreb, 25 February 1993

* This number includes 32,000 registered refugees from other Republics of former Yugoslavia but not an estimated 93,000 unregistered refugees.
† This number rises to about three million with the inclusion of some one million additional persons also assisted by UNHCR.

(R) = registered   (E) = estimated   n/a = not available displaced persons and people trapped in war zones—have now been directly affected and are dependent on external aid in Bosnia-Herzegovina and other republics of Yugoslavia. About 600,000 are in other European countries, notably Germany (see Table 9). More than 100,000 have been killed. The scale of the operation—both humanitarian and peacekeeping—is twice that which the international community faced in Iraq two years ago and the largest undertaking of its kind to date.

What has happened is that humanitarianism has had to move far out ahead of politics. The Security Council and other UN member nations have used humanitarianism as a substitute for what in other times would have been treated as political and military problems.[102] Instead of coming from governments and other official bodies, the leadership for drawing attention to the plight of victims of conflict

TABLE 9
**Estimated Asylum-Seekers from Ex-Yugoslavia
in Other European Countries**

Host Country	Number	Comments
Germany	250,000	asylum-seekers, vulnerable groups, and others
Switzerland	80,000	
Austria	73,000	registered asylum-seekers and de facto refugees & non-registered
Sweden	62,202	
Hungary	40,000	one-third are registered and assisted by the Hungarian Government
Turkey	18,060	
Italy	16,000	
Czech Republic & Slovakia	10,000	
Denmark	7,323	asylum-seekers and vulnerable groups
The Netherlands	5,995	registered (7,000 including non-registered)
Spain	4,654	asylum-seekers and vulnerable groups
Great Britain	4,424	asylum-seekers
France	4,200	
Others	46,200	
TOTAL	**595,080**	

Source: UNHCR Geneva, February 1993

and state deterioration, both in ex-Yugoslavia and Somalia, has devolved to humanitarian organizations and relief workers, whose witness, catalogued by the media, has mobilized public opinion to demand official attention.

In the process, humanitarian agencies have been thrown into the midst of conflict, unarmed and vulnerable, in situations where in the past they would have been evacuating their personnel. It is true that an international presence is, in itself, a potent tool of protection. But there are limits to what humanitarian action and presence can accomplish; those limits have been dramatically exceeded in ex-Yugoslavia and Somalia.

Moreover, ex-Yugoslavia demonstrates that efforts to concentrate on the country of origin can also become a way to bottle up genuine refugees in their own country, rationalizing that they do not require asylum in other places because humanitarian agencies have been dispatched to the source. This is a dangerous tendency inherent in country-of-origin strategies, important and urgent though they are. The offer of asylum and temporary refuge must always be available as a genuine option for refugee emergencies. Relief agencies should not be required to operate in a milieu of life-threatening conditions combined with closed borders, so that virtual case-by-case negotiation becomes necessary to help victims who cannot be helped in place.

The new themes elicited by the case of ex-Yugoslavia include the following:

- A legal framework and institutional mandate for assistance and protection to potential refugees who are internally displaced is becoming more urgent as the international community focuses refugee prevention efforts upon countries of origin.

- By necessity, relief has become linked with military efforts, and peacekeeping doctrine is being broadened to include protecting supplies for delivery to civilians.

- Opportunities for asylum and temporary refuge in developed countries have been severely restricted, heightening the importance of refugee prevention initiatives focused on countries of origin.

For Europe and the NATO alliance, the absence of a perceived strategic interest in the Yugoslavian conflict has allowed it to escalate to the point where the scale of the refugee emergency now constitutes, in and of itself, a security threat to the region.

D. HAITI

Since the mid-1970s, Haiti has produced mixed flows of migrants characteristic of flows that developed in many parts of the world during the 1980s. To contain the boat departures, the United States negotiated an agreement with Haiti to interdict at sea. Boat people were brought aboard U.S. Coast Guard cutters, cursorily interviewed for refugee status, and returned to Haiti.[103] Cubans, who also often took to boats to get to the United States, are the beneficiaries of both a special exception in U.S. law that grants them residence within one year of arrival and a policy of non-return to a Communist country. The contrast has become increasingly stark and indefensible.

In 1991, the first democratic elections in Haiti's history were followed by a military coup. With it came a sharp escalation in political violence. A surge of boat departures ensued, overwhelming the ability of officials to rescue and interview the growing numbers of people. To contain the spiraling emergency, President Bush ordered all boat people to be picked up and returned without interviews. Simultaneously, the United States was decrying the overthrow of Haiti's democracy and the lawlessness of the coup leaders, and giving strong backing to the Organization of American States (OAS) in its diplomatic initiatives to overturn the coup and impose a trade embargo.

The contradiction was not lost on Bill Clinton, whose campaign position was that Haitians deserved fair interviews. Such is the power and reach of mass communications that with his election, Haitians began building boats in anticipation of a policy change that they interpreted as an invitation to come to the United States. As the incoming Administration contemplated the potential for a boat crisis just as it was taking office, a serious review of Haitian policy became a priority.

The policy the Clinton Administration is pursuing targets the conditions that produce irregular migration, while also offering refugee resettlement for individuals who are threatened. Its essential features are:

- Working with the OAS and the UN, establish an international human rights presence in Haiti to quell egregious human rights abuses. After much negotiation, Haitian officials agreed to this initiative, and 500 monitors have been dispatched to the island.

- Give strong support and assistance to the UN special envoy's efforts to negotiate a diplomatic solution that provides for the return of Haiti's elected President and begins to build democratic political processes.

- Expand in-country processing of refugee applicants so that centers are available at several locations throughout the country. This provides people who are immediately threatened with a way to apply for resettlement in the United States as an alternative to dangerous boat journeys.

The new themes evoked by the Haiti case include the following:

- Unregulated, emergency migrations to developed countries, even when they may include genuine refugees, are being treated as a threat that requires priority foreign policy attention.

- Traditional migration problems are triggering broader political initiatives that target the underlying causes of flight.

The importance being attached to Haiti by the new Administration demonstrates how differently security and national interests may begin to look in a post-Cold War setting. Nations like Haiti, that have not been of any strategic interest to major Trilateral powers, except to be kept non-Communist, are beginning to demand attention because their poverty and oppression generates instability that can spark sizeable migrations. Such emergency, unregulated migrations can, in turn, undermine the well-being of neighboring states.

*   *   *

The "hope and hazard" of our times is giving rise to themes that, taken together, constitute significant departures for migration policy thinking and execution, at least in the realm of humanitarian activity. Conditions on the ground are expanding the role of international humanitarian agencies into areas beyond their mandates and experience. The changing ways migration questions are presenting themselves and being addressed have consequences for a full spectrum of heretofore fixed notions, from perceptions of sovereignty to definitions of national interest.

Although attention to issues surrounding refugee flows has shifted dramatically to solutions anchored in country-of-origin strategies, it is also clear that country-of-origin policies standing alone are as inadequate as was asylum, when it served as the sole avenue of international response. Country-of-origin spending now commands an important share of UNHCR's budget, and donors have been responsive to funding appeals. Thus, there has been exceptionally keen awareness of the need to attack refugee problems at the source.

Yet increasing proportions of humanitarian funding are being devoted to security requirements for relief workers and the delivery of supplies, rather than to refugees themselves. This points to the need for balance and for utilizing and nurturing a range of policy responses, including asylum opportunities.

Refugee issues have insinuated themselves onto the international political agenda and governments are looking to the UN system to address refugee crises, just as they are asking the UN to undertake dramatically expanded roles in peacekeeping, human rights monitoring, peace negotiations, organizing elections, etc. But the UN is itself, in the end, an instrument of its member-governments, which must provide the needed political and financial support. Their commitment and ability to confront tomorrow's problems today will determine the final outcomes.

VI. WHERE DO WE GO FROM HERE?: A FRAMEWORK FOR POLICY

The causes of contemporary migrations are deeply embedded in the social, economic and political conditions of our times. Yet to the extent that nations have migration policies at all, most handle them as narrow, particularistic functions. To be effective, policy must go beyond conventional control and humanitarian measures, so that managing migration pressures becomes part of nations' central economic, political and security objectives.

Comprehensive policies that address the causes of political and economic migrations will require a fundamental shift in the outlook and actions of Trilateral states. That shift should be anchored in a new international imperative, the right of individuals to stay where they are. Most international migration today is an act of desperation, not choice. The vast majority of individuals prefer home and will stay there, if conditions are even barely tolerable. It is that impulse that policy must build on. Freedom of movement should reflect options and choice; it should not be the sole avenue for survival.

Even if "the right to stay" guides international action, developed countries face growing immigration pressures for the foreseeable future and must move aggressively to manage them more effectively. Responsible opinion leaders should avoid generating hysteria by characterizing migration as an "invasion" or "flood." Compassionate policies toward refugees must be preserved and defended. Transparency in migration policy-making must be more conscientiously pursued to inform public opinion and combat racism and xenophobia, which are endemic problems that can be overcome only by education and by insisting that democratic principles of tolerance and equal treatment be practiced.

A broad consensus is developing in Trilateral countries that receiving countries must be attentive to pre-refugee, pre-migration circumstances in sending countries. Conflict prevention and other political and assistance initiatives must be mobilized quickly and early to prevent them from becoming crises. In some circumstances, sizeable emergency migrations can even constitute legitimate security concerns, when they undermine the well-being of receiving countries. Thus, migration prevention is a legitimate objective of international diplomacy and national policy.

This consensus should also spark policy-making that goes to the reasons people migrate. This requires a broad mix of national, regional and international measures that embrace political and economic objectives. To those ends, we recommend the following:

• **Nations must develop policies and systems for effective integration of newcomers who have already arrived and for the orderly admission of immigrants and refugees whose contributions fulfill important national purposes.**

The most pressing migration challenge for Trilateral countries begins at home. As the pre-eminent global powers, these nations must be self-confident, successful societies in order to provide the leadership, innovation and financing necessary to address international migration pressures. Successfully integrating existing populations of newcomers is a prerequisite for responding more broadly and forcefully to the longer-term demands of international migration trends.

The most important measure of successful immigrant integration is inter-generational economic progress. Such progress has an important political dimension as immigrants become a disproportionately larger part of the younger, working population of societies whose ageing native populations will draw heavily upon publicly financed social welfare programs. Targeting the children of immigrants is, therefore, particularly important.

States have an obligation to control entry into their societies. They should do so by establishing reasoned admissions policies for labor market, refugee, and family immigrant groups, along with firm, judicious enforcement regimes that deny entry to those who do not qualify. Most developed nations have sound reasons to invite some foreigners to join the society. Examining and debating those reasons and developing policy accordingly will contribute importantly to improved migration regulation and control.

Reform of political asylum decision-making is of special importance. Asylum decisions must be timely and perceived to be fair. The volume of cases will diminish if there are other legitimate avenues of entry to a country. Although the sources and circumstances for refugee flows are changing, substantial numbers will continue to require protection, humane treatment, and, in some cases, resettlement in other countries. Developed nations have become excessively legalistic and narrow in their interpretation and use of the 1951 Convention Relating to the Status of Refugees and its 1967 Protocol, the only legally binding international instruments governing migration matters. The asylum crisis has further crippled the ability of some to respond compassionately. Nations must take more generous stances on asylum and refugee questions, including finding ways to provide temporary refuge under some circumstances, if an international regime of effective refugee protection is to survive and have meaning.

- **An international migration regime must evolve and be fostered.**

The UNHCR is the crisis arm of international efforts to handle migration problems, but there is very little else that is comprehensive and coordinated. An international migration regime would consist of new legal instruments and the operational capacity to respond to the full range of international migration situations. This capacity should be institutionalized in the way the International Monetary Fund (IMF) or the General Agreement on Tariffs and Trade (GATT) operate where monetary and trade policies are concerned. Such a regime of international principles and institutions would touch a range of areas including the following:

Asylum-seekers should be treated similarly across national boundaries. The concept—embodied in the Dublin Convention and under discussion by Canada and the United States—of binding arrangements wherein nations accept the asylum decisions of other nations should be pursued and extended. A critical feature of such arrangements over time will be that national authorities incorporate international standards and scrutiny in their decision-making.

Internally displaced people raise difficult questions of jurisdiction for the international community when governments are no longer willing or able to fulfill the most rudimentary requirements of protection for their nationals. Great care must be exercised in defining the issues. However, displacement borne of conflict situations where populations are on both sides of international borders might legitimately trigger international action. To date, international responses have been case-by-case, bolstered by individual Security Council resolutions to authorize international involvement. The review of the UNHCR mandate in 1994 provides an appropriate opportunity to examine this issue and develop a broad, collective view of how to treat future cases.

Humanitarian intervention is becoming a new international legal principle which is dramatically changing traditional understandings of sovereignty. Trilateral countries should endorse the idea that violence within a country of groups dedicated to destroying or displacing one another can constitute a threat to international peace and security. Nevertheless, the bases for international interventions in such cases must be incorporated into carefully developed standards and judgments, collectively made, regarding human rights and civil violence thresholds whose violation would trigger various forms of intervention.

Coordination and enhancement of UN functions must be focused more effectively on ameliorating the causes of migrations. The newly created office of the Undersecretary for Humanitarian Affairs can be a strong focal point for rationalizing the work of disparate UN agencies whose mandates encompass migration questions. Delineating the organizational and policy linkages between the human rights, humanitarian assistance, and economic development functions and capacities of the UN system are areas of critical importance. Having called for automatically available forces for peacekeeping purposes, a proposal governments should support, the Secretary-General must also establish the command and logistics capability required to deploy such forces.

The UN Convention on the Rights of Migrant Workers and Their Families must be debated and ratified by states. If the objections of developed countries to the Convention cannot be overcome, another instrument speaking to the issues of human rights and analogous protections for workers and their families who are outside their countries of nationality must be developed. Because these are drawn-out processes, intermediate measures, such as addressing labor standards in the context of trade agreements like the NAFTA, must be pursued.

These are all ingredients of an international migration regime. There are many more that are in various stages of development or that must be originated to provide a viable international framework within which to manage migration pressures effectively.

• Foreign policies and international priorities must emphasize broad-based improvements in human rights conditions and democracy.

Vast numbers of people do not enjoy the most fundamental protections in their societies. Human rights initiatives have tended to concentrate on exposing individual crimes and cases of dissidents or groups that are persecuted. The focus must broaden to include overall conditions of justice and free political participation, regardless of whether particular governments are friend or foe, with the objective of changing conditions that deprive large numbers of people of basic rights and freedoms. This is of particular importance with regard to the protection of minorities and minority rights, which must be treated as a fundamental tenet in the evolution of democratic states.

International human rights institutions must also be considerably strengthened, if goals of democratic development are to be realized. At present, UN human rights bodies are limited to standard-setting activities and have no operational capacity to assist countries in implementing international norms. The proposal for a UN High Commissioner on Human Rights, advanced at the 1993 World Conference on Human Rights in Vienna, could represent a significant move toward the strengthening that is needed.

The end of the Cold War has given way to democratic elections or peace agreements in countries from Estonia to El Salvador. They need help in establishing impartial judicial procedures, professional police and military forces, and vibrant non-governmental sectors. International assistance in building the habits and institutions of democracy in newly liberated states is central to preventing ruinous migrations.

• Population stabilization and sustained development must be aggressively pursued in the countries which now house the majority of the world's population.

Development policies that provide some measure of economic hope for individuals and nations without stimulating substantial new migrant flows are a threshold challenge for the international community.

Population policy is a first-order priority. The decade of the 1990s presents the last chance for action if world population is to be stabilized by the middle of the next century. With the change of administrations in the United States, a major philosophical shift in official attitudes has occurred which should be the basis for renewed American leadership. Family planning services in developing countries could provide contraception to almost 60 percent of women of reproductive age by 2000 if current funding is simply doubled from $4-5 billion to $9 billion.[104] These are not large sums and the benefits are incalculable.

The percentage of national budgets devoted to military spending has taken limited resources away from needed social spending in many countries in both the developed and developing worlds. However, the military/non-military balance has been particularly distorted in many high-emigration countries. IMF estimates are that a one percent reduction in defense spending internationally would free up $140 billion. This would more than compensate for shortages in capital to devote to development and human resources investments.

Trilateral countries must also engage in constructive regionalism to bridge the migration rifts that skirt their national or regional perimeters. Targeted development policies aimed at upgrading living standards in Mexico—enacting NAFTA is of particular importance in that regard—and the Caribbean, the Maghreb, and Eastern Europe will go a long way toward establishing viable zones that will assist in managing migration pressures. Such policies require important trade-offs, however. The very products most likely to be competitively produced by less developed countries are often those which advanced countries continue to protect. Migration pressures are centrally affected by this standoff. Successfully concluding the Uruguay Round of the GATT is an important step toward overcoming some of the barriers that inhibit job creation in developing economies.

These examples illustrate that solid, attainable development goals are within reach. Nations and the international community need to establish precise targets for action and commit to achieving them. Only cooperative, multilateral efforts that include aid, trade and investment can have an impact on the poverty that leads not only to unhealthy migrations, but to political and social upheaval.

*   *   *

Movements of people are challenging fundamental concepts of the state which date back many centuries. The dilemmas can no longer be seen as a problem for a few nations, for democracies are being drawn ever closer by the common external circumstances we face. Nor can nations afford to act alone as individual gatekeepers trying to build higher and higher walls. International migration—along with global trade, environmental degradation, drugs and terrorism, and weapons proliferation—is a new fact of national and international life that requires new kinds of cooperation among all nations.

Appendices
and Notes

APPENDIX A
Refugees and Asylum-Seekers in
Need of Protection and/or Assistance
(as of December 31, 1992)

Host Country Country of Origin		Host Country Country of Origin	
AFRICA: 5,698,450			
Malawi	**1,070,000**	**Uganda***	**179,600**
Mozambique	1,070,000	Sudan	90,000
		Rwanda*	83,300
Sudan*	**750,500**	Zaire	4,000
Ethiopia/Eritrea*	730,000	Somalia	2,100
Chad*	14,500	Other	500
Uganda	4,000		
Zaire	2,000	**Zambia**	**155,700**
		Angola	118,000
Guinea*	**485,000**	Mozambique	24,000
Liberia*	385,000	Zaire	9,000
Sierra Leone*	100,000	South Africa	700
		Other	4,000
Zaire	**442,400**		
Angola	280,000	**Burundi***	**107,350**
Sudan	120,000	Rwanda*	81,000
Burundi	17,000	Zaire	26,000
Rwanda	13,000	Other	350
Uganda	10,000		
Other	2,400	**Liberia**	**100,000**
		Sierra Leone	100,000
Kenya*	**422,900**		
Somalia*	320,000	**Djibouti**	**96,000**
Ethiopia	80,000	Somalia	85,000
Sudan	20,000	Ethiopia	11,000
Rwanda	2,200		
Uganda	700	**Senegal**	**55,100**
		Mauritania	55,000
Ethiopia/Eritrea*	**416,000**	Other	100
Somalia*	400,000		
Sudan	16,000	**Swaziland**	**52,000**
		Mozambique	45,000
Zimbabwe*	**265,000**	South Africa	7,000
Mozambique*	264,000		
Other	1,000		

Tanzania	**257,800**
Burundi	143,000
Mozambique	72,000
Rwanda	22,300
Zaire	16,000
Somalia	1,200
Other	300
South Africa*	**250,000**
Mozambique*	250,000
Algeria*	**210,000**
Western Sahara*	165,000
Mali	35,000
Niger	5,000
Palestinians	5,000
Cote d'Ivoire	**195,500**
Liberia	195,000
Other	500

Mauritania	**40,000**
Mali	40,000
Rwanda	**24,500**
Burundi	24,000
Zaire	500
Central African Republic	**18,000**
Sudan	17,000
Chad	1,000
Ghana	**12,100**
Liberia	10,000
Togo	2,000
Other	100
Guinea-Bissau	**12,000**
Senegal	12,000
Egypt	**10,650**
Somalia	5,600
Palestinians	4,400
Ethiopia	400
Other	250

MIDDLE EAST: 5,586,850

Iran*	**2,781,800**
Afghanistan*	2,700,000
Iraq	81,800
Jordan	**1,010,850**
Palestinians	1,010,700
Other	150
Gaza Strip	**560,200**
Palestinians	560,200
West Bank	**459,100**
Palestinians	459,100
Lebanon	**322,900**
Palestinians	319,400
Other	3,500

Syria	**307,500**
Palestinians	299,200
Iraq	6,400
Somalia	1,900
Iraq	**64,600**
Iran	64,000
Other	6000
Yemen	**52,500**
Somalia	49,000
Ethiopia	3,4000
Other	100
Saudi Arabia	**27,400**
Iraq	27,400

EUROPE AND NORTH AMERICA: 3,423,600

Serbia/Montenegro* Former Yugoslavia*	**621,000** 621,000	**Ukraine***	**40,000**
		Canada	**37,700**
Germany Former Yugoslavia Other	**536,000** 220,000 316,000	**Macedonia*** Former Yugoslavia* Other	**32,700** 32,500 200
Russian Federation	***460,000**		
		Turkey Former Yugoslavia Iraq Iran	**31,700** 20,000 10,300 1,400
Croatia* Former Yugoslavia*	**420,000** 420,000		
Armenia* Azerbaijan*	**300,000** 300,000	**France** Former Yugoslavia Other	**29,400** 4,200 25,200
Azerbaijan* Armenia* Other	**246,000** 195,000 51,000	**Netherlands** Former Yugoslavia Other	**24,600** 7,000 17,600
United States Haitians (Guantanamo) Other	**103,700** 300 103,400	**United Kingdom** Former Yugoslavia Other	**24,600** 4,900 19,700
Sweden Former Yugoslavia Other	**88,400** 74,000 14,400	**Belgium** Former Yugoslavia Other	**19,100** 3,400 15,700
Austria Former Yugoslavia Other	**82,100** 73,000 9,000	**Italy** Former Yugoslavia Other	**19,100** 17,000 2,100
Switzerland Former Yugoslavia Other	**81,700** 70,000 11,700	**Denmark** Former Yugoslavia Other	**13,900** 7,000 6,900
Bosnia and Hercegovina Former Yugoslavia*	***70,000** 70,000	**Spain** Former Yugoslavia Other	**12,700** 4,600 8,100
Slovenia* Former Yugoslavia*	**68,900** 68,900		
Hungary Former Yugoslavia	**40,000** 40,000		

SOUTH AND CENTRAL ASIA: 2,341,700

Pakistan	**1,577,000**	**Bangladesh**	**245,300**
Afghanistan	1,575,000	Burma	245,000
Other	2,000	Other	300
India*	**378,000**	**Nepal**	**89,400**
Sri Lanka	181,000	Bhutan	75,400
China (Tibet)	114,000	China (Tibet)	14,000
Bangladesh*	50,000		
Bhutan*	20,000	**Afghanistan**	**52,000**
Afghanistan	11,000	Tajikistan	52,000
Burma	2,000		

EAST ASIA AND THE PACIFIC: 398,600

Thailand	**255,000**	**Malaysia**	**16,700**
Cambodia	129,000	Vietnam	10,300
Burma	72,000	Burma	4,700
Laos	40,800	Indonesia	1,700
Vietnam	12,600		
Other	600	**Indonesia**	**15,600**
		Vietnam	15,000
Hong Kong	**45,300**	Cambodia	600
Vietnam	45,300		
		China*	**12,500**
Australia	**24,000**	Burma*	10,000
		Laos	2,500
Vietnam	**19,000**		
Cambodia	19,000		

LATIN AMERICA AND THE CARIBBEAN: 107,700

Mexico	**47,300**	**Costa Rica**	**34,350**
Guatamala	44,000	Nicaragua	27,850
El Salvador	2,600	El Salvador	5,600
Other	700	Cuba	250
		Other	650

GRAND TOTAL: 17,556,900

Source: U.S. Committee for Refugees, *1993 World Refugee Survey* (Washington: USCR, 1993), pp. 50-51.

Note: Refugees and asylum seekers who require international protection and/or assistance are unable or unwilling to repatriate due to fear of persecution and violence in their homelands. This table does not include refugees permanently settled in other countries. In some cases, refugees listed in the table may no longer require assistance, but still need international protection. The table excludes countries hosting 10,000 or fewer persons. A companion USCR table lists "selected populations in refugee-like situations," totalling another roughly 4 million individuals at the end of 1992.

* indicates that sources vary significantly in the number reported

APPENDIX B
Declaration on Principles of Governing External Aspects of Migration Policy

12 December 1992
European Community Edinburgh Summit
(European Council of Heads of State
and Government of the European Community)

i)   The European Council, meeting at Edinburgh, discussed the question of migratory pressures.

ii)   It noted with satisfaction that profound political changes now permit greater ease of travel and contacts throughout Europe.

iii) It reaffirmed its intention to ensure that the Community and its Member States remain open to the outside world, not only through personal and cultural exchanges, but also through their commitment to a liberal trading system, by playing their full part in assisting the developing world, and by establishing a framework of political and economic relations with third countries and groups of third countries. In this, the European Council reaffirms the principles of its Declaration at Rhodes in December 1988.

iv)   The Member States of the European Communities reaffirmed their commitment to honour in full their obligations under the 1950 European Human Rights Convention, the 1951 Geneva Convention on the status of refugees and the 1967 New York Protocol.

v)   It was conscious of the particular pressures caused by the large movements of people fleeing from the conflict in the former Yugoslavia particularly given the harsh winter conditions.

vi)   It noted the pressures on Member States resulting from migratory movements, this being an issue of major concern for Member States, and one which is likely to continue into the next decade.

vii) It recognized the danger that uncontrolled immigration could be destabilizing and that it should not make more difficult the integration of third country nationals who have legally taken up residence in the Member States.

viii) It stressed the need to reinforce the fight against racism and xenophobia in line with the joint declaration adopted by the European Parliament, the Council and the Representatives of the Member States, meeting within the Council, and the Commission on 11 June 1986 and with the Declaration on racism and xenophobia adopted by the European Council in Maastricht.

ix)   It was convinced that a number of different factors were important for the reduction of migratory movements into the Member States: the preservation of peace and the termination of armed conflicts; full respect for human rights; the creation of democratic societies and adequate social conditions; a liberal trade policy, which should improve economic conditions in the countries of emigration. Co-ordination of action in the fields of foreign policy, economic co-operation and immigration and asylum policy by the Community and its Member States could also contribute substantially to addressing the question of migratory movements. The Treaty on European Union, notably its Titles V and VI, once in force, will provide an adequate framework for this co-ordinated action.

x)   It took note of the declaration adopted on the occasion of the Development Council on 18 November 1992 on aspects of development co-operation policy in the run-up to 2000, including the recognition of the role which effective use of aid can make in reducing longer term migratory pressures through the encouragement of sustainable social and economic development.

xi)   It noted that, in line with the views of the United Nations High Commissioner for Refugees, displaced people should be encouraged to stay in the nearest safe areas to their homes, and that aid and assistance should be directed towards giving them the confidence and the means to do so, without prejudice to their temporary admission also in the territory of Member States in cases of particular need.

xii) It welcomed the progress made by Ministers with responsibility for Immigration matters under the work programme endorsed at the Maastricht European Council, and in particular the adoption of recommendations on expulsion, resolutions on manifestly unfounded applications for asylum and on host third countries and conclusions on countries in which there is generally no serious risk of persecution.[1] It recognized the importance of such measures against the misuse of the right of asylum in order to safeguard the principle itself.

xiii) It also welcomed the work on east-west migration of the Berlin and Vienna Groups, and encouraged the Berlin Group to prepare a draft resolution for agreement by Ministers.

xiv) It resolved to take forward those more general migration-related issues set out in the Maastricht work programme that go wider than the direct responsibilities of the Ministers with responsibility for Immigration matters.

---

[1]The resolutions on manifestly unfounded applications for asylum and on host third countries and the conclusions on countries in which there is generally no serious risk of persecution have been accepted by Germany under the reservation of a modification of her fundamental law, and by Denmark and the Netherlands subject to a Parliamentary scrutiny reservation.

xv) It recognized the importance of analyzing the causes of immigration pressure, and analyzing ways of removing the causes of migratory movements.

xvi) It agreed that the approach of the Community and its Member States, within their respective spheres of competence, should be guided and informed by the following set of principles:

1. they will continue to work for the preservation and restoration of peace, the full respect for human rights and the rule of law, so diminishing migratory pressures that result from war and oppressive and discriminatory government;

2. displaced people should be encouraged to stay in the nearest safe area to their homes, and aid and assistance should be directed towards giving them the confidence and the means to do so without prejudice to their temporary admission also in the territory of Member States in cases of particular need;

3. they will further encourage liberal trade and economic co-operation with countries of emigration, thereby promoting economic development and increasing prosperity in those countries, and so reducing economic motives for migration;

4. to the same end, they will ensure the appropriate volume of development aid is effectively used to encourage sustainable social and economic development, in particular to contribute to job creation and the alleviation of poverty in the countries of origin, so further contributing in the longer term to a reduction of migration pressure;

5. they will reinforce their common endeavours to combat illegal immigration;

6. where appropriate, they will work for bilateral or multilateral agreements with countries of origin or transit to ensure that illegal immigrants can be returned to their home countries, thus extending co-operation in this field to other States on the basis of good neighbourly relations;

7. in their relations with third countries, they will take into account those countries' practice in readmitting their own nationals when expelled from the territories of the Member States;

8. they will increase their co-operation in response to the particular challenge of persons fleeing from armed conflict and persecution in former Yugoslavia. They declare their intention to alleviate their plight by actions supported by the Community and its Member States directed at supplying accommodation and subsistence, including in principle the temporary admission of persons in particular need in accordance with national possibilities and in the context of a co-ordinated action by all the Member States. They reaffirm their belief that the burden of financing relief activities should be shared more equitably by the international community.

xvii) The European Council urges those Members States who have not already done so to ratify the Dublin Asylum Convention as part of their co-ordinated action in the field of asylum; it will then be possible to extend such arrangements under a convention parallel to the Dublin Convention, giving priority to neighbouring European countries where these arrangements could be mutually beneficial. The European Council calls for the necessary action to be taken so that the External Frontiers Convention can come into effect at an early date.

APPENDIX C
1951 Convention Relating to the Status of Refugees
(excerpts)

The High Contracting Parties...

Considering that it is desirable to revise and consolidate previous international agreements relating to the status of refugees and to extend the scope of and the protection accorded by such instruments by means of a new agreement,

Considering that the grant of asylum may place unduly heavy burdens on certain countries, and that a satisfactory solution of a problem of which the United Nations has recognized the international scope and nature cannot therefore be achieved without international co-operation,...

Article 1
Definition of the term "Refugee"

A. For the purposes of the present Convention, the term "refugee" shall apply to any person who:

(2) As a result of events occuring before 1 January 1951 and owing to well-founded fear of being persecuted for reasons of race, religion, nationality, membership of a particular social group or political opinion, is outside the country of his nationality and is unable or, owing to such fear, is unwilling to avail himself of the protection of that country; or who, not having a nationality and being outside the country of his former habitual residence as a result of such events, is unable or, owing to such fear, is unwilling to return to it....

C. This Convention shall cease to apply to any person falling under the terms of section A if:...

(5) He can no longer, because the circumstances in connexion with which he has been recognized as a refugee have ceased to exist, continue to refuse to avail himself of the protection of the country of his nationality;...

Article 2
General obligations

Every refugee has duties to the country in which he finds himself, which require in particular that he conform to its laws and regulations as well as to measures taken for the maintenance of public order....

Article 3
Non-discrimination

The Contracting States shall apply the provisions of this Convention to refugees without discrimination as to race, religion or country of origin....

Article 17
Wage-earning employment

1. The Contracting State shall accord to refugees lawfully staying in their territory the most favourable treatment accorded to nationals of a foreign country in the same circumstances, as regards to right to engage in wage-earning employment....

Article 32
Expulsion

1. The Contracting States shall not expel a refugee lawfully in their territory save on grounds of national security or public order....

Article 33
Prohibition of expulsion or return ("refoulement")

1. No Contracting State shall expel or return ("refouler") a refugee in any manner whatsoever to the frontiers of territories where his life or freedom would be threatened on account of his race, religion, nationality, membership of a particular social group or political opinion....

Article 34
Naturalization

The Contracting States shall as far as possible facilitate the assimilation and naturalization of refugees. They shall in particular make every effort to expedite naturalization proceedings and to reduce as far as possible the charges and costs of such proceedings....

Article 35
Co-operation of the national authorities with the United Nations

1. The Contracting States undertake to co-operate with the Office of the United Nations High Commissioner for Refugees, or any other agency of the United Nations which may succeed it, in the exercise of its functions, and shall in particular facilitate its duty of supervising the application of the provisions of this Convention....

1967 Protocol Relating to the Status of Refugees
(excerpts)

The States Parties to the present Protocol,

Considering that the Convention relating to the Status of Refugees done at Geneva on 28 July 1951 (hereinafter referred to as the Convention) covers only those persons who have become refugees as a result of events occurring before 1 January 1951,

Considering that new refugee situations have arisen since the Convention was adopted and that the refugees concerned may therefore not fall within the scope of the Convention,

Considering that it is desirable that equal status should be enjoyed by all refugees convered by the definition in the Convention....

Have agreed as follows:

Article I

1. The States Parties to the present Protocol undertake to apply...the Convention to refugees as hereinafter defined.

2. ...the term "refugee" shall...mean any person within the definition of article 1 of the Convention as if the words "As a result of events occurring before 1 January 1951 and..." and the words "...as a result of such events" in article 1 A(2) were omitted.

3. The present Protocol shall be applied by the States Parties hereto without any geographic limitation....

APPENDIX D
Security Council Resolution 688 (April 1991)
(excerpts)

The Security Council,

Mindful of its duties and its responsibilities under the Charter of the United Nations for the maintenance of international peace and security,

Recalling Article 2, paragraph 7, of the Charter of the United Nations,

Gravely concerned by the repression of the Iraqi civilian population in many parts of Iraq, including most recently in Kurdish populated areas which led to a massive flow of refugees towards and across international frontiers and to cross border incursions, which threaten international peace and security in the region,

Deeply disturbed by the magnitude of the human suffering involved,...

Reaffirming the commitment of all Member States to the sovereignty, territorial integrity and political independence of Iraq and of all States in the area...

1. *Condemns* the repression of the Iraqi civilian population in many parts of Iraq, including most recently in Kurdish populated areas, the consequences of which threaten international peace and security in the region;

2. *Demands* that Iraq, as a contribution to removing the threat to international peace and security in the region, immediately end this repression and expresses the hope in the same context that an open dialogue will take place to ensure that the human and political rights of all Iraqi citizens are respected;

3. *Insists* that Iraq allow immediate access by international humanitarian organizations to all those in need of assistance in all parts of Iraq and to make available all necessary facilities for their operations...

NOTES

Chapter I
Who Are Today's Migrants? Why Are They on the Move?

1. Remarks by Lawrence Eagleburger, former U.S. Secretary of State, at a televised meeting of the Council on Foreign Relations, Washington, D.C., January 7, 1993.
2. This includes almost 3 million persons legalized under the terms of the Immigration Reform and Control Act of 1986 (IRCA).
3. Sadako Ogata, "Refugees: A Humanitarian Strategy," Statement before the Royal Institute for International Relations, Brussels, November 25, 1992.
4. Anthony Lake et al., *After the Wars: Reconstruction in Afghanistan, Indochina, Central America, Southern Africa and the Horn of Africa*, U.S.-Third World Policy Perspectives No. 16, Overseas Development Council (New Brunswick: Transaction Publishers, 1992).
5. For a more complete discussion of these phenomena and their characteristics, see Astri Suhrke, "Towards a Comprehensive Refugee Policy: Conflict and Refugees in the Post-Cold War World," Chr. Michelson Institute, Bergen, Norway, prepared for the UNHCR/ILO Joint Meeting in Geneva, May 6-8, 1992, revised July 1992.
6. Gil Loescher, *Refugee Movements and International Security*, Adelphi Paper 268 (London: International Institute for Strategic Studies, 1992).
7. Suhrke, *Comprehensive Refugee Policy*, p. 18.
8. For a fuller discussion of this point, see Saskia Sassen, *The Global City: New York, London, Tokyo* (Princeton: Princeton University Press, 1991).
9. Michael Teitelbaum, "The Population Threat," *Foreign Affairs* 71:5 (Winter 1992-93), and Sharon L. Camp, "Population: The Critical Decade," *Foreign Policy* 90 (Spring 1993).
10. Teitelbaum, "The Population Threat."
11. Sharon Stanton Russell and Michael S. Teitelbaum, "International Migration and International Trade," World Bank Discussion Paper No. 160 (Washington, D.C.: The World Bank, 1992).

Chapter II
Canada and the United States

12. Robert L. Bach and Doris M. Meissner, *America's Labor Market in the 1990s: What Role Should Immigration Play?* (Washington, D.C.: Carnegie Endowment for International Peace, June 1990).
13. Other provinces have begun to consider negotiating similar autonomous arrangements.
14. Quebec has exercised this right since 1978 with increasing autonomy. In 1991, an agreement with Canada outlined provisions that allow it to preserve its own demographic and cultural identity with regard to immigration. With the exception of family immigrants and some humanitarian admissions, it has sole responsibility for the selection of the immigrants intending to live in Quebec and for administering its own reception and social, cultural, and economic integration programs. For more on this subject see Demetrios G. Papademetriou, "International Migration in North America: Issues, Policies,

Implications," Paper prepared for the Joint UN Economic Commission for Europe/UNFPA meetings in Geneva, July 1991, p. 37.

15.   In 1962, government regulations overturned the historic "whites only" policy, though certain advantages remained for European admissions. Such advantages were completely eliminated in the 1967 legislation. For more on this subject, see Papademetriou, "International Migration in North America", and F. Hawkins, *Critical Years in Immigration: Canada and Australia Compared* (Montreal: McGill-Queens's University Press, 1989).

16.   Papademetriou, "International Migration in North America."

17.   Canadian admissions for business reasons produced $3 billion of investment from 1986 to 1990. The program is seen to be an unqualified success story. It is credited with providing 10 percent of Canada's investment growth during that period, 6.3 percent of its net increase in full-time employment, and 3 percent of total growth in GDP. Among the favored investment activities are accommodations; food and beverages; manufacturing of clothing and textiles, followed by food, plastics, and electrical and electronic products; retail; construction; and wholesale. See Papademetriou, "International Migration in North America," and R. Kunin, "The Economic Impact of Business Immigration Into Canada," Employment and Immigration Canada, Regional Economic Services Branch BC/YT, September 1991.

18.   Rosemary Jenks, ed., *Immigration and Nationality Policies of Leading Migration Nations* (Washington, D.C.: Center for Migration Studies, 1992), p. 5.

19.   Family members are: spouses and unmarried children, never-married children over 18 years of age and their dependents, parents, grandparents over 60 (widowed or incapable of working) and their children, siblings, nephews and nieces, and grandchildren under 18 years of age who were never married and orphaned. See Papademetriou, "International Migration in North America."

20.   Papademetriou, "International Migration in North America," and Meyer Burstein, "Canadian SOPEMI Report, 1991," Paris, OECD, 1991.

21.   Papademetriou, "International Migration in North America," and Burstein, "Canadian SOPEMI Report, 1991."

22.   Jenks, *Immigration and Nationality Policies.*

23.   Legislation approved in 1993 (and noted later in the main text) has modified this procedure somewhat. Positive decisions from both members are required for claimants who arrive without documentation, who are nationals of a country such as the United States, or who return to the country where they claim to be in danger while their claims are pending. For more on this subject, see "Managing Immigration: A Framework for the 1990s," Employment and Immigration Canada, July 1992.

24.   The broader question raised by the cost and effort that is now absorbed by Canada's system is one of proportionality. Given the vast numbers of refugees in the world and the tremendous needs they represent, is it defensible that a rich nation spends large amounts of money to admit but 55,000 individuals each year?

25.   "Backgrounders to the Annual Report to Parliament: Immigration Plan for 1991-1995," Employment and Immigration Canada, October 1990.

26.   Just under 9 million arrived during the 1980s, exceeding the previously

highest decade of 1901-1910 by about 100,000 people. Of the 1980s total, 7.34 million arrived as permanent residents. The remainder have adjusted their status from that of temporary resident alien, which was granted through the legalization program enacted by Congress in 1986. At the turn of the century, the percentage of foreign-born in the population was 14 percent, as compared with 8 percent today. Canada, in comparison, has a foreign-born population of 16.1 percent today. See Jenks, *Immigration and Nationality Policies.*

27. Immediate relatives of U.S. citizens are defined as minor children (under age 21), spouses, parents of U.S. citizens over age 21 and widows and widowers of U.S. citizens. There is no numerical restriction on the number of these relatives of citizens who can enter the country each year. Therefore, there are no serious delays to their coming. Family members who are subject to numerical limitations and may, therefore, face longer delays in immigrating are adult unmarried children of U.S. citizens, spouses and minor children of permanent residents, adult sons and daughters of permanent residents, married sons and daughters of citizens, and siblings of adult citizens. See Jenks, *Immigration and Nationality Policies.*

28. U.S. Immigration & Naturalization Service, *Statistical Yearbook of the Immigration & Naturalization Service, 1991* (Washington, D.C.: U.S. Government Printing Office, 1992).

29. With the end of the Cold War, the border between Germany and Central European states may be analogous. The difference in population growth rates, however, remains a unique factor where Mexico and the United States are concerned.

30. The actual number of people apprehended is not captured by apprehension statistics which simply record an enforcement action. Because illegal Mexicans are promptly turned back to Mexico, many try again, making multiple entries until they succeed. Thus, considerably less than 1.6 million *persons* are likely to have been intercepted.

31. See "GAO Advises Clinton on Transition Issues," *Interpreter Releases* 70: 3 (January 15, 1993).

32. The Refugee Act of 1980 gives refugees immediate access to certain types of support, including transportation, relocation allowances, job training, and domestic safety-net programs (such as Aid to Families with Dependent Children [AFDC], Supplemental Security Insurance, and Medicaid). However, Congress has been unwilling to sustain its commitment to absorbing much of the costs of eligibility for these programs. Between 1982 and 1990, resettlement assistance fell from $4,500 per refugee to $2,000, and the federal government reduced its reimbursement support to state and local governments for public assistance and AFDC from 36 months to 12 months and 4 months, respectively. For more on this subject, see Elizabeth S. Rolph, *Immigration Policies: Legacy from the 1980s and Issues for the 1990s* (Santa Monica, CA: RAND Corporation, 1992).

33. Michael Fix, "Remarks before the Commission on Immigration Reform," The Urban Institute, January 5, 1993.

34. *Final Report of the Commission for the Study of International Migration and Cooperative Economic Development* (Washington, D.C.: U.S. Government Printing Office, 1990).

35.   Dolores Acevedo and Thomas J. Espenshade, "Implications of a North
       American Free Trade Agreement for Mexican Migration into the United
       States," *Population and Development Review* 18:4 (December 1992), pp. 729-744.
36.   While the critical issue for the potential migrant is wage differentials,
       productivity differentials are also critical for a potential investor
       choosing between the United States and Mexico. Wages are much
       higher in the United States, but so is productivity.
37.   Acevedo, "Implications for Mexican Migration," p. 735.

Chapter III
European Community Countries

38.   William Pfaff, "Reflections: The Absence of Empire," *The New Yorker*
       (August 10, 1992).
39.   Max Wingen, "Immigration to the Federal Republic of Germany as a Demo-
       graphic and Social Problem," paper delivered at the "International
       Conference on Mass Migration in Europe: Implications for East and
       West," March 5-7, 1992, Vienna. In Germany, for example, by
       September 1990, 27 percent of the foreigner population was composed
       of EC citizens. That percentage had been over 50 percent in the second
       half of the 1960s; by 1970, it fell below 50 percent and reached less than
       one-third during the 1980s.
40.   Jonas Widgren, "The Need to Improve Co-Ordination of European
       Asylum and Migration Policies," remarks delivered before the
       Conference of the Trier Academy of European Law on "Comparative
       Law of Asylum and Immigration in Europe," March 12-13, 1992.
41.   Most of the illegals appear to be concentrated on the pressure points of
       Europe's boundaries: in the East (Austria and Germany) and the South
       (Italy, Spain, Portugal and Greece). Of the 2.7 million foreign
       population of the latter countries, about half are believed to be illegal
       immigrants and this number is expected to rise to about three million
       by the year 2000. In 1987-88, there were thought to be 850,000 illegals in
       Italy, 294,000 in Spain, 70,000 in Greece, and 60,000 in Portugal.
            Minimal past estimates come from the response to "regularization"
       programs. Such programs in France in 1981 yielded 132,000
       regularizations of illegals, 118,000 in Italy in 1987, and 44,000 in Spain
       in 1985. Those regularized were mostly North Africans.
            Other minimal indications come from apprehensions and
       deportations. In the United Kingdom, for example, in 1990, 3,293
       persons were dealt with as illegal entrants, about three times the
       number ten years earlier. Estimates of the UK total have never been
       published but European comparisons suggests it is unlikely to be less
       than 100,000. See D.A. Coleman, "Report to the European Population
       Conference," United Nations Geneva, March 23-26, 1993.
42.   In France, statistics distinguish between the foreign-born, who are also
       called immigrants, and foreigners, who include French-born children
       (6.3% of the population) of foreign parents who have not been
       naturalized. Over half of France's immigrants came from Portugal
       (18%), Algeria (17%), and Morocco (16%). Substantial numbers have
       also come from Italy, Spain, Tunisia, and Turkey. For Germany, the
       main source countries of the foreign born population are Turkey (30%),

Yugoslavia (12.3%) Italy (8.8%), Greece (5.8%) and Portugal (4.7%). See Jenks, *Immigration and Nationality Policies.*

43. Figures developed by the Intergovernmental Consultation on Asylum, Refugee and Migration Policies in Europe, North America and Australia, a group of 16 OECD countries, as reported in "Refugees: Keep Out," *The Economist,* September 19, 1992.

44. Much of this analysis was provided in an unpublished essay, entitled "A U.S. Perspective on Migration Issues in Europe," by Priscilla Clapp and Princeton Lyman, Senior Deputy Assistant Secretary and Director, respectively, of the Bureau for Refugee Programs, Department of State, February 1992.

45. Luise Drüke, "Asylum in a European Community without Internal Borders: New Opportunities and Risks in the Post-Cold War Europe," paper prepared for a meeting on "Critical Issues in International and United States Refugee Policy," Fletcher School of Law & Diplomacy, Tufts University, November 1992.

46. Richard Layard, Oliver Blanchard, Rudiger Dornbusch, and Paul Krugman, *East-West Migration: The Alternatives* (Cambridge: MIT Press, 1992), as described in "Before the Flood," *The Economist,* November 28, 1992.

     Polling data released by the EC Commission in March 1993 showed that in East-Central Europe, the Baltics, Ukraine, and European Russia, 1.2 percent (2.7 million) declared the firm intention to emigrate and 7.3 percent (16.7 million) declared they would "certainly" or "probably" leave.

47. President Ben Ali of Tunisia (who is also President-in-Office of the Arab Maghreb Union), in a June 22, 1993 speech to the European Parliament, proposed the elaboration of a Euro-Maghreb Charter which would define the rights and duties of immigrants from the Maghreb countries to the European Community. See *Agence Europe,* June 22 and 23, 1993.

48. Widgren, "Co-Ordination of European Policy."

49. Applications pending figures provided by Ruprecht von Arnim, Regional Representative, UNHCR, Brussels. See "Deputies Face Protests as Bonn Debates Asylum Laws," *Financial Times,* May 22, 1993. See also "German Lawmakers, Amid Threats, to Vote on Asylum Bill," *Washington Post,* May 26, 1993.

50. The annual numbers are as follows: in 1988, 203,000; in 1989, 720,000; in 1990, almost 400,000; and in 1991, about 222,000. As cited in Clapp and Lyman, "Migration Issues in Europe."

51. Resettlers from the ex-GDR continue to leave their homes at the rate of about 10,000 per month. Since the opening of the Wall in November 1989, about 1.1 million have come to western Germany.

52. "Youths Adrift in a New Germany Turn to Neo-Nazis," *New York Times,* September 28, 1992; "Disabled Germans Fear They'll be the Next Target," *New York Times,* January 19, 1993; and "Turks Death Dash Optimism in Germany," *Washington Post,* May 31, 1993.

53. "Turks Death Dash Optimism in Germany," *The Washington Post,* May 31, 1993.

54. Some officials have confronted violence aggressively. The Interior Minister of Saxony established a Special Commission on Rightist Extremism which solved 92 percent of the violent crimes that had been committed in his jurisdiction. The number of attacks quickly fell by

almost half. See "Germany Blocks a Big Neo-Nazi Rally Near Berlin," *New York Times*, November 16, 1992.

55. The groups are the Nationalist Front, an organization of about 130 members whose platform calls for the expulsion of all foreigners, and the German Alternative. In addition, the Republican Party, a far-right party with more than 25,000 members and elected representatives in several state and local legislatures, was barred from holding a recent convention in Hannover on the grounds that the meeting would have "endangered the public security and order." See "Germany Outlaws a Neo-Nazi Group," *New York Times*, November 28, 1992; and "Germany Moves to Ban a Second Neo-Nazi Party," *New York Times*, December 11, 1992.

56. "Acceptance Urged of Germans: President Criticizes Anti-Foreigner Acts," *Washington Post*, December 25, 1992.

57. "Germany's Turks Erupt with Pent-up Anger," *Washington Post*, June 2, 1993.

58. "Bonn Ends Asylum Right," *Washington Post*, May 27, 1993.

59. "Bonn Ends Asylum Right," *Washington Post*, May 27, 1993.

60. He noted that more than one-third of restaurant workers, half of metalworkers and 70 percent of street cleaners are foreigners.

61. "Acceptance Urged of Germans: President Criticizes Anti-Foreigner Acts," *Washington Post*, December 25, 1992.

62. Edith Cresson in France; leader of Denmark's swing party discussing the vote against the Maastricht Treaty. See "Schluter in Fight to Beat 'Tamilgate'," *Financial Times*, January 13, 1993; and "What German Crisis?," *The New Republic*, December 21, 1992.

63. "Germany's Turks Erupt with Pent-up Anger," *Washington Post*, June 2, 1993.

64. Among the many sources that treat European integration processes, this section draws upon two relatively short summaries that are straightforward and very helpful in understanding the migration aspects of Europe-wide activity. They are Jacqueline Bhabha, "Harmonization of European Immigration Law," *Interpreter Releases* 70:2 (January 11, 1993); and Giuseppe Callovi, "Regulation of Immigration in 1993: Pieces of the European Community Jig-Saw Puzzle," *International Migration Review* 26:2 (Summer 1992).

65. The Schengen Group originally included France, Germany, Belgium, Luxembourg, and the Netherlands. It has been expanded to include Portugal, Spain, Italy, and Greece.

66. Norway, Sweden, Finland, Iceland, Liechtenstein, and Austria.

67. That is, as long as the Court of Justice will not have interpreted Article 8a of the Maastricht Treaty. The EC Commission's interpretation of Article 8a has held that "[t]he complete abolition of physical frontiers for individuals exercising their right to freedom of movement necessarily implies the complete abolition of controls on all individuals who cross internal borders, irrespective of their nationality. Any other interpretation of the objective of abolishing physical frontiers would render Article 8a ineffective. If, after 31 December 1992, Member States are still able to check whether a person wishing to cross a border is a national of a Member State and whether he or she constitutes a danger to public order, public security or public health, nothing will have

changed and Article 8a will be dead letter." "Communication of the European Commission on the lifting of internal border controls in the EC on January 1st, 1993," Brussels, 6 May 1992.

68. Exceptions can be made for persons who have close connections in a country other than the one first entered.

69. The Treaty classified issues as either areas of Community competence or areas of intergovernmental jurisdiction. Under the three "pillars" established by the Treaty, the first pillar covers Community matters. Visa questions are now part of that pillar. The second pillar is for defense and foreign policy and does not touch upon migration issues. The third pillar, for intergovernmental matters, includes the bulk of the issues on the migration agenda that are under discussion among states in Europe today.

70. The expectation for the Maastricht meeting was that the European Council would make a commitment in the Treaty to "formal and actual harmonization" of policies of asylum, immigration and aliens, bringing activities currently carried on in an intergovernmental framework into the sphere of the Union. The Commission prepared two documents, one on the right of asylum, another on immigration, to that end. However, the proposals fell prey to the impulses to protect national will and individuality that surrounded the entire Maastricht effort.

The intergovernmental approach for migration policy-making is consistent with past practice. It began in 1986 with the creation of an ad hoc Immigration Group within the Secretariat of the EC Council to prepare the necessary actions for implementing the Single Market. Because of the delicacy of the issues from the standpoint of national sovereignty, the recommendation called for the bulk of necessary actions to be taken at the intergovernmental, instead of the Community level. Since then, the Group has developed both the Dublin and External Borders Conventions. It has never ruled out the possibility, however, of consensus developing over the limitation of the intergovernmental approach or the desirability of further harmonization and coordination. For more on this subject, see Callovi, "Regulation of Immigration."

71. The force of these agreements depends on whether they are adopted as resolutions, which require member states to bring their national laws into conformity by a specified date, or as recommendations and conclusions, which have less force.

72. France, Germany, Italy, Spain, Portugal, Belgium, Netherlands and Luxembourg.

73. Denmark, Greece, United Kingdom, Italy, and Portugal.

74. The integration process is a theme that has not been discussed in this chapter for lack of space. Briefly, Europe has relied on four differing integration approaches. France pursues an assimilationist model. Britain has favored a multicultural or pluri-ethnic society. Germany uses neither of these but is slowly easing very strict naturalization laws. The Netherlands and Nordic countries promote extensive and expensive integration into the economy in an effort to enable immigrants to contribute.

European unification and migration policy-making proceed with these differing models in operation, all of them in serious crisis, as illustrated by disproportionately high rates of non-EC citizen unemployment.

75. Article K4 of the Maastricht Treaty provides for a Coordinating Committee, which will succeed the Ad Hoc Immigration Group. A group of senior officals, the K4 Committee, will continue to prepare policies for member state ratification. The work of the Ad Hoc Group has, in fact, been quite structured and formal. It has met regularly for six years and is organized into five subgroups. They are Admission/Expulsion; Asylum; External Frontiers; False Documents; and Visas. For more on this subject, see Bhabha, "Harmonization of European Immigration Law."

76. For example, there are two efforts, known as the Berlin and the Vienna processes, that are cross-national exchanges initiated by the German and Austrian governments, respectively. They have established working groups, meet regularly, etc. Although there are some distinctions, the substantive issues are not fundamentally different from Schengen group or External Borders Convention matters.

77. Germany also negotiated an agreement with Romania in September 1992 that eases return of Gypsies.

78. This too requires Constitutional change. Article 116 provides the right to immigrate without numerical limitations. The number who came in 1991 was 220,000. With the 10 percent formula, this means that up to 242,000 admissions in this category could be made each year.

79. "Kohl Explains Absence from Turks' Funeral," *Washington Post,* June 8, 1993.

80. The German citizenship law was adopted in 1913 during a period of deep nationalism when ideas of racial purity were widely accepted. Children born in Germany are not automatically citizens, even if both parents were also born there. Thus, there exist second and third generation foreigners, a contradiction in terms for North Americans, for example. For those who are eligible, naturalization is a complex and costly process. Fees can exceed $3,000. The residence requirement to apply is 15 years, or eight years (including six years attendance in a German school) for those under age 23. Screening by police officials results in most applications being rejected for reasons that include traffic violations. Frequently, the reasons are unspecified, leading to the widely held suspicion that a bias against political activity is applied. Such practices are in sharp contrast with the treatment of ethnic Germans who get virtually automatic citizenship, without expense or exhaustive background checks. See "German Law Won't End Immigration Problems," *New York Times,* January 9, 1993; and "Germans Plan to Make it Easier for Some to Obtain Citizenship," *New York Times,* January 25, 1993.

Chapter IV
Japan

81. Japan's population of 123 million includes 1.2 million foreigners. The largest minority are Koreans, who number about 700,000. Many were brought forcibly when Japan occupied their homeland. Although in Japan for generations, they have faced persistent discrimination on many fronts in Japanese society. For example, to insure public security,

they had to be fingerprinted in order to work, study and live in Japan. The change eliminating this procedure from the Alien Registration Law became effective in January 1993. See "Low-cost, Illegal Foreign Workers Boon for Business, Worry for Society: Labor Shortage, High Wages Spur Rapid Influx," *The Nikkei Weekly*, August 1, 1992.

82. "Let Foreign Laborers Stay and Work if Trained, Panel Urges," *The Nikkei Weekly*, December 14, 1991.

83. Demetrios G. Papademetriou, "Japan and Migration," Report prepared for the Carnegie Endowment for International Peace Board of Trustees, November 1992.

84. "New Law Stirs Migrant Worker Issue," *The Japan Economic Journal*, June 9, 1990.

85. Papademetriou, "Japan and Migration."

86. "New Law Stirs Migrant Worker Issue," *The Japan Economic Journal*, June 9, 1990.

87. In Japanese, the three "Ks"—Kitsui, Kitanai, Kiken.

88. "Japan and International Migration: Challenges and Opportunities," a seminar jointly sponsored by the Geneva-based International Organization for Migration (IOM) and the Tokyo-based Association for the Promotion of International Cooperation, October 1992.

89. "Record Number of Foreigners Denied Entry into Japan," *The Nikkei Weekly*, July 4, 1992; and "Safeguards Needed to Assure Fair Deal for Foreign Labor; Exploitation Serves Neither Japan nor Employers," *The Nikkei Weekly*, October 5, 1992.

90. "'Answer to Influx of Illegal Workers is Aid,' says White Paper: Creation of Jobs in Home Countries Urged," *The Nikkei Weekly*, April 11, 1992.

91. "New Law Stirs Migrant Worker Issue," *The Japan Economic Journal*, June 9, 1990.

92. Things are not working out as well as planned. The Latin American Japanese are frequently subjected to the same exploitative working conditions as illegal workers, they often do not speak Japanese, and their cultural outlook and habits are decidedly Latin despite their appearance and heritage. Their status is called "long-term resident," which is the same status as that of Koreans and Vietnamese in Japan. See "Latin American 'Nisei' Fill Labor Shortage: Other Foreign Workers Flee Tough New Law," *The Japan Economic Journal*, December 8, 1990.

93. "Current Growth Rates, Greater International Role Expected," *The Nikkei Weekly*, April 25, 1992.

Chapter V
The International Community and Refugees:
Different Contexts, Changing Approaches

94. A number of international organizations concern themselves with various aspects of either economic or political/refugee migration. They include the Organization for Economic Cooperation and Development (OECD), which publishes statistics and analysis on economic and integration aspects of immigration in advanced industrial societies; the International Labour Organization (ILO), which has concentrated its research heavily on contract labor and economic development

questions; and the International Organization for Migration (IOM), which has information programs for migrants, carries out repatriation and reintegration programs for skilled labor, and helps states develop immigration legislation and programs.

95. About two-thirds went to Iran, which kept open its borders; one-third massed at the Turkish-Iraqi border, trapped in rugged mountains in wet, freezing weather. Although the large majority were Kurds, who fled north and east, about 70,000 Shia refugees also fled to Iran, and 30,000 Iraqis in the south were under the care of Coalition forces. See "Statement to the Trilateral Commission by Mrs. Sadako Ogata, UN High Commissioner for Refugees," April 22, 1991, published in *Tokyo 1991: The Annual Meeting of the Trilateral Commission* (New York: 1991).

96. Turkey also believed it had assurances of resettlement that had not been met for a few thousand Kurds who had fled to Turkey from Iraqi gas attacks two years earlier and were still languishing in camps with no prospects of relocation.

97. Sadako Ogata, "Refugees: A Humanitarian Strategy," Statement before the Royal Institute for International Relations, Brussels, November 25, 1992.

98. Iain Guest, "Returning Refugees in Cambodia—The Development Gap," An Opinion Paper (Washington, D.C.: The Refugee Policy Group, October 15, 1992).

99. Frederick C. Cuny, Barry N. Stein and Pat Reed, eds., *Repatriation During Conflict In Africa and Asia* (Dallas: Center for the Study of Societies in Crisis, 1992).

100. Relief within countries has traditionally been provided by the International Committee of the Red Cross (ICRC).

101. These ideas are set forth in several of Mrs. Ogata's public statements made in October and November 1992 to the UNHCR's Executive Committee; the Royal Institute for International Relations in Brussels; at the Peace Palace, The Hague; and to the Trilateral Commission European Group meeting in Dublin.

102. An interesting example of the downgrading that has occurred in governments' interests in humanitarian crises comes from France. An interlocutor reports that humanitarian causes that were once given high priority for official funding by the government are now the object of elaborate donation drives, as if the only devotion they merit is charity, voluntarily expressed by citizens.

103. Between 1981 and the end of 1990, of the more than 20,000 Haitians intercepted and interviewed at sea, only six were found to have a basis for a refugee application and were brought to the United States for more thorough interviewing. See "Cast Away," *The American Lawyer,* October 1992.

Chapter VI
Where Do We Go From Here?: A Framework for Policy

104. *Changing Our Ways: America and the New World,* Carnegie Endowment National Commission on America and the New World (Washington, D.C.: Carnegie Endowment for International Peace, July 1992).